Pocket
Technica

CW01019590

The Hierar
in Arc

The laws of thermodynamics – and their implications for architecture – have not been fully integrated into architectural design. Architecture and building science too often remain constrained by linear concepts and methodologies regarding energy that occlude significant quantities and qualities of energy.

The Hierarchy of Energy in Architecture addresses this situation by providing a clear overview of what energy is and what architects can do with it. Building on the emergy method pioneered by systems ecologist Howard T. Odum, the authors situate the energy practices of architecture within the hierarchies of energy and the thermodynamics of the large, non-equilibrium, non-linear energy systems that drive buildings, cities, the planet, and the universe.

Part of the *PocketArchitecture* series, the book is divided into a fundamentals section, which introduces key topics and the emergy methodology, and an applications section, which features case studies applying emergy to various architectural systems. The book provides a concise but rigorous exposure to the system boundaries of the energy systems related to buildings and thus will appeal to professional architects and architecture students.

Ravi Srinivasan is Assistant Professor of Low / Net Zero Energy Buildings at the College of Design, Construction and Planning at the University of Florida, USA. He develops and teaches new courses related to low and net zero energy buildings in both the undergraduate and graduate programs, enhancing the School's internationally recognized sustainable construction management program, researching and establishing net zero and low energy building frameworks, and organizing student competitions. He has more than 50 technical publications in peer-reviewed journals, refereed conference papers, and research reports.

Kiel Moe is Associate Professor of Architecture and Energy at the Graduate School of Design at Harvard University, USA, where he is Co-Director of the MDes program, Co-Coordinator of the Energy & Environments MDes concentration, and Co-Director of the Energy, Environments, and Design Research Unit. He is author of *Insulating Modernism: Isolated and non-isolated thermodynamics in architecture* (2014), *Convergence: An architectural agenda for energy* (2013), *Thermally Active Surfaces in Architecture* (2010), and *Integrated Design in Contemporary Architecture* (2008). He was co-editor, with Ryan Smith, of *Building Systems: Design technology & society* (2012).

PocketArchitecture:
Technical Design Series

Series Editor: Ryan E. Smith

Building Information Modeling
Karen M. Kensek

Life Cycle Assessment
Kathrina Simonen

Daylighting and Integrated Lighting Design
Christopher Meek and Kevin Van Den Wymelenberg

Architectural Acoustics
Ana M. Jaramillo and Chris Steel

The Hierarchy of Energy in Architecture
Ravi Srinivasan and Kiel Moe

PocketArchitecture:
Technical Design Series

The Hierarchy of Energy in Architecture

Emergy analysis

**Ravi Srinivasan and
Kiel Moe**

Routledge
Taylor & Francis Group

LONDON AND NEW YORK

First published 2015
by Routledge
2 Park Square, Milton Park, Abingdon, Oxon OX14 4RN

and by Routledge
711 Third Avenue, New York, NY 10017

Routledge is an imprint of the Taylor & Francis Group, an informa business

British Library Cataloguing in Publication Data
A catalogue record for this book is available from the British Library

Library of Congress Cataloging-in-Publication Data
Srinivasan, Ravi.
The hierarchy of energy in architecture energy analysis / Ravi Srinivasan and Kiel Moe.
    pages cm. – (Pocketarchitecture: technical design series)
    Includes bibliographical references and index.
    1. Buildings – Thermal properties. 2. Architecture and
    energy conservation. 3. Buildings – Energy conservation.
    I. Moe, Kiel. II. Title.
    TH1715.S676 2015
    720′.472 – dc23   2014045560

ISBN: 978-1-138-80352-7 (hbk)
ISBN: 978-1-138-80353-4 (pbk)
ISBN: 978-1-315-75367-6 (ebk)

Typeset in Goudy and Univers
by Florence Production Ltd, Stoodleigh, Devon, UK
Printed and bound in Great Britain by Ashford Colour Press Ltd, Gosport, Hampshire

"The full transition to a renewable economy will only become possible when architects understand the different qualities of the materials, power sources, and settlement patterns with which they work. In *The Hierarchy of Energy*, Srinivasan and Moe explain the concepts and tools needed for environmental building design, and situate architecture within the self-organization of human and natural ecosystems."

– Dr. William W. Braham, FAIA, Director,
Master of Environmental Building Design,
University of Pennsylvania, USA

Contents

Figures

Tables

All images by the authors, except where noted.

Series editor's preface

Although architects and building professionals come into contact with, specify, design, and build technical practices every day, they actually know relatively little about them. They are "abstract systems" construed and constructed upon industry norms passed through generations of professionals. Most of them are correct, but many, when disassociated from their cultural underpinnings of building vernacular and, more importantly, their scientific basis and practice contexts, present challenges that cause buildings not to perform as intended or, worse, lead to physical, economic, or social catastrophe.

PocketArchitecture: Technical Design Series fills this void. The series comprises succinct, easy-to-use, topic-based volumes that collate in one place unbiased, need-to-know technical information about specific subject areas by expert authors. This series demystifies technical design criteria and solutions. It presents information without overladen theory or anecdotal information. *PocketArchitecture* is on point.

As the name would suggest, the volumes in this series are pocket sized and collectively serve as a knowledge base on technical subjects in architecture, creating a value-added information base for building novices and masters alike. In addition to architects, engineers, and contractors who deliver building projects, the series is appropriate for students and academics interested in accessible technical information as it relates to building design and construction.

Despite their size, the series volumes are highly illustrated. Furthermore, the volumes use easily accessible language to succinctly explain the fundamental concepts and then apply these basic ideas to cases of common issues encountered in the built environment. *PocketArchitecture* is essential, accessible, and authoritative. This makes it important reading for architectural technologists, architects, building surveyors, building commissioners, building engineers, other construction professionals, and even owners and clients.

This volume, *The Hierarchy of Energy in Architecture: Emergy analysis*, is concerned with holistic energy considerations in the built environment. As opposed to linear and reductivist thinking concerning energy, this volume, building on the work of ecologist Howard T. Odum on emergy, presents a systems-based approach to energy in architecture. It is a non-linear, complex, and more inclusive perspective on energy hierarchies in buildings. However, it is accessible, practical, and applied. As part of the *PocketArchitecture Series* the book includes both fundamentals and advanced topics. It is appropriate for the novice and expert practitioner as its content is fresh and well considered in the field of texts on energy architecture.

Preface

The energy systems related to human life, buildings, cities, and civilization are not adequately incorporated into architecture. In the prevailing forms of analysis in architecture, such as energy analysis or life cycle assessment, important forms of energy and essential energetic processes are methodologically externalized. As a result, architecture and engineering routinely construe curious system boundaries for the energy systems associated with buildings and often focus on the wrong magnitudes of energy. They routinely treat buildings as small scale, steady-state, isolated thermodynamic systems when in fact buildings are large scale, transient, and open thermodynamic systems. Buildings are lodged in a nested hierarchy of energy exchange, and, without understanding a building's dynamic in these hierarchies, we will not ever devise ways for buildings to maximize their impact on the environment and develop the maximum power systems that drive all forms of life and all processes on this planet. Currently designers operate without understanding the hierarchy of energy in buildings and the relative order of magnitudes associated with these hierarchies. Understanding the relative power of these magnitudes of energy is essential for design in the twenty-first century.

In short, designers need to ask critical questions about the system boundaries of every project in order to identify the maximal intake, transformation, use, storage, and feedback of the energy required of buildings. What is, what should be, the system boundary of a particular building project? These most basic thermodynamic questions about system boundaries must address the full spatial and temporal flux of energy that presupposes a building. The most rigorous and totalizing forms of energy accounting originated in ecological systems analysis: The thermodynamic analysis of large scale systems. Buildings and cities are large scale energy systems and so these ecosystem analysis methodologies offer great insight regarding the energy systems of buildings. In view of this, in this book we situate building in the context of these comprehensive forms of analysis.

To understand this method, we must present key concepts that help articulate the system boundaries of a building and, in doing so, articulate how this methodology differs in scope from other, more familiar forms of analysis. We then present a couple of examples of thorough emergy analysis. The first is a simplified system – a mobile information kiosk. This simplified system will allow the reader to grasp the method. The second example focuses on a large institutional building and thus provides insight on the relative magnitudes of energy involved in buildings and their hierarchies of energy. We then also provide key citations and resources on this important emerging aspect of building science and design.

Part 1

Fundamentals

chapter 1

Energy, entropy, exergy, and emergy

1.0 Energy systems

TO UNDERSTAND EVEN THE MOST RUDIMENTARY aspects of the energy systems inherent to architecture requires an expanded, if not new, set of vocabulary and concepts. To cogently act on the purpose and potential of design in the context of energy demands an even more exacting vocabulary and conceptual understanding of energy systems. The aim of this chapter is to introduce the intricate concepts and structures of energy systems as a basis for design. Without a broad introduction, the structure, behavior, and purpose of energy systems will remain abstract and unknown to designers.

Currently, the term energy is widely used in confusing, obfuscating, and incomplete ways (Figure 1.1). It is used as an overly generalized term to describe an enormous range of processes and concepts for which there is a more precise vocabulary. To clarify understanding, it is necessary to grasp the roles and relationships of the following four terms: energy, entropy, exergy, and emergy (spelled with an "m").

In this context, emergy – the focus of this book – in particular, is a most revealing concept. The concept of emergy developed in ecosystem science and offers a more totalizing description of the thermodynamics of large scale energy systems such as buildings and cities. Emergy is a contraction of "energy memory," and this contraction offers a hint about the more broad system boundaries of its concern. Given the systemic origin of this term, emergy most fully articulates the many implications of thermodynamics in the context of architecture and urbanization. Often misunderstood as a type of embodied energy analysis, emergy is the best way to gain a comprehensive understanding of energy systems. One of its primary contributions is the way in which it radically clarifies and illustrates the actual dynamics of energy systems. Its relevance, then, is both instructive and methodological insight into the hierarchies of

ENERGY CONSISTS OF
MULTIPLE FORMS AND TYPES
[SUBSETS] OF ENERGY.

AN ENERGY
DISCOURSE & PRACTICE
REQUIRES MORE EXACTING
VOCABULARY AND
CONCEPTS.

1.1 Energy is an umbrella term for far more specific terms

energy and relative orders of magnitude that constitute the energy systems of architecture.

For many readers, emergy might appear as a new term. Other readers, with mixed exposure to the term and its use, might benefit from a clear explication of the term and its uses. All readers, we hope, will benefit from both the concept and the example applications of emergy analysis in this book. Our aim is to help articulate more powerful and efficacious agendas for energy in architecture. Emergy is an important conceptual and practical tool towards this end.

To understand the many implications of energy, entropy, exergy, and emergy, it is first necessary to review some fundamental aspects of energy systems and their universal thermodynamic tendencies. The first section of this chapter will thus restate some of the basic principles of energy systems that are routinely absent from energy system considerations in architecture and urbanization. This first section will thus focus on the structure and behavior of energy systems.

Systems and boundaries

All energy systems consist of the following structure: **a system, its boundary, and its surroundings**. The system is a portion of the universe – a body, a building, a planet – that is the focus of concern. Everything that surrounds that system is its surroundings (Figure 1.2). The boundary that separates the system and its surroundings varies and must be situationally determined. The boundary is less an object than a stated type of exchange, a change in behavior, or a shift of energetic activity pertinent to the analysis at hand. Thus it is critical to select a relevant system boundary that simplifies, but does not over-simplify, the system and its exchanges with its surroundings. In this regard, designers must develop the habit of routinely asking, "What is my system boundary, and why?"

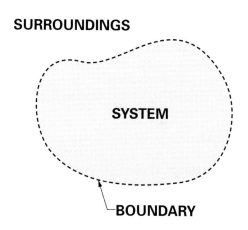

1.2 Energy system components

The selection of a system boundary – and what it does and does not encompass spatially and temporally – is one of the most consequential design decisions for energy systems. Yet, it remains one of the least considered decisions in current energy methodologies. Without an awareness and adequate definition of the system boundary, it is very common to ignore or externalize consequential energetic exchanges and relationships. Given the potential magnitude of this systemic error, not understanding the system boundary might undermine the very purpose of energy system analysis and design.

Open, closed, or isolated

Depending on the selected system boundary, an energy system will either be designated as open, closed, or isolated. These categories stipulate the type of interaction between a system and its surroundings. Each boundary type identifies if any matter and/or energy is exchanged between the system and its surroundings.

An **open system** will exchange both matter and energy across the boundary (Figure 1.3). Human bodies, buildings, and cities are examples of open systems. Each of these open systems will exchange many forms of matter and energy over time with its surrounding milieu. Bodies, buildings, and cities not only exist and survive as open systems, but also thrive as open systems. Especially as open systems, it is important to ask, however, what is the system boundary of a body or a building? There are multiple appropriate systems boundaries that all depend on the type of inquiry guiding the analysis. The energetic exchanges of a body or a building, for example, extend well beyond their respective skin and envelope systems. What should be considered inside the system and what should surround the system? How the system boundary is construed greatly impacts the relevance and significance of the analysis or design. In this way, current energy system design in architecture frequently suffers unconsidered or inadequate system boundary definition.

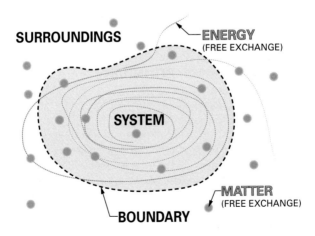

1.3 An open thermodynamic system

A **closed system** will exchange energy, but not matter, across a boundary (Figure 1.4). A hermetically sealed glass jar of water is a closed system. One can add or remove heat from the jar system but the quantity of matter inside the jar system will remain constant. There are phases of a building – such as construction or demolition – when the exchange of matter is perhaps paramount. There are other phases – such as in the amount of solar energy gained in a greenhouse in a four-hour period – when just the exchange of energy is paramount. The latter can be considered a closed system for the stated boundary period, *but only* for that stated time period.

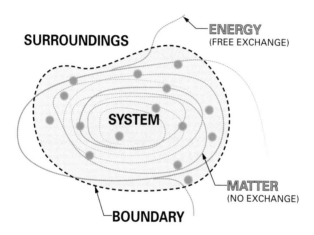

1.4 A closed thermodynamic system

An **isolated** system exchanges neither energy nor matter across the boundary (Figure 1.5). It is difficult to construe system boundaries wherein a building is understood to exchange no matter or energy. The universe as a whole is most likely an isolated system. Isolated systems often only exist as conceptual abstractions and there are few actual isolated systems. For instance, the most common statement of the second law of thermodynamics – that a system tends towards maximum entropy – presumes an isolated system. It is extremely important to recognize, however, that all buildings and urbanization exist as non-isolated systems.

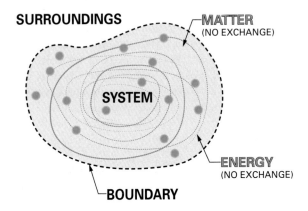

1.5 An isolated thermodynamic system

With the basic system-surrounding structure of energy systems in place, it is possible to consider more directly the laws of thermodynamics that govern the behavior of all energy system structures.

1.1 Thermodynamic laws

WITHOUT EXCEPTION, ENERGY SYSTEMS follow a set of universal tendencies. Over the past two centuries, scientists in a range of disciplines have observed energy system principles and dynamics that are so consistent and inviolable as to be deemed universal "laws." (For familiarity, we'll maintain this metaphor of law-based system governance, even though there is no juridical entity that adjudicates system tendencies.) The zeroth law establishes the concept of heat and its equivalence in all energy systems. The third law establishes the concept of absolute zero, the theoretical minimum possible energy state. The first and second of these laws, in particular, bear consideration.

The first law of thermodynamics states that energy can be neither created nor destroyed. This is the conservation of energy. All energy is conserved. It is therefore by definition confusing to claim that a particular design aims to "conserve energy." This outcome is spontaneously guaranteed regardless of the design. Likewise, it is impossible to "produce" energy in a building or otherwise. Rather, energy is only transformed or converted to other forms and states. The construction and occupation of a building requires the transformation of many forms of energy. This fact is a very valid premise for the design of energy systems, whereas frequent references to the "production" or "conservation" of energy in a building through design simply do not have any thermodynamic correspondence in reality.

The second law states that isolated systems tend toward a state of equilibrated matter and energy. The universe, you see, abhors available energy gradients and forms emerge that degrade those gradients. A fully equilibrated system would fully degrade available gradients. Such systems would have maximum entropy. Maximum entropy means that all available energy gradients in a system have been dissipated and the system is completely homogenous. Thus, as entropy increases, the energetic potential energy of an isolated system will be less than its initial state. In other words, as energy dissipates in a system, the quantity of energy in a system remains the same but the qualities of energy in a system do not remain constant.

To paraphrase systems ecologist Howard T. Odum, these thermodynamic laws can be summarized as follows: Energy will be maintained and conserved (the first law), but its capacity to do work, however, will not be maintained (the second law)[1] (Figure 1.6). It is the qualitative change of energy states evident in the latter half of this statement that proves most consequential for energy systems and design. It is the implications of the second law that have great consequence for design.

A perceived linear relationship in many statements of the second law for isolated systems often leads to equally linear, and thus erroneous, motivations

FIRST LAW:
Energy will be conserved.

SECOND LAW:
The capacity of energy to do work will not be conserved.

1.6 Restated primary laws of thermodynamics

for efficiency and conservation designs. But, again, buildings are non-isolated systems. Isolated and non-isolated systems behave in very different ways. This difference between isolated and non-isolated systems is inordinately consequential. While an isolated system will run down to a state of zero potential or maximum entropy, through the exchange of matter and energy a non-isolated system can persist or even thrive. In short, these systems are in a state far from equilibrium. The implications of this fact are vast for the design of the non-isolated energy systems that constitute architecture and urbanization. These implications are elaborated in the second half of this chapter.

With the basic energy system structure and laws in place, the distinction of the terms energy, entropy, exergy, and emergy will have more clear significance. The next section of this chapter expands on each of these terms.

1.2 Energy, entropy, exergy, and emergy

Energy

ENERGY, BY DEFINITION, REFLECTS the capacity of a system state to do work on its surroundings. Energy is measure of work capacity. Power refers to the rate at which this work is done. The specificity of the mechanisms by which this work is done, and its vocabulary, are essential to an understanding of energy systems. It is extremely important that designers develop this basic energetic literacy so that both pedagogy and practice can finally begin to more fundamentally align with reality.

As pointed out at the beginning of this chapter, the term energy is often used in a very general way that obfuscates reality. This creates great confusion and unfortunate energy system designs. For example, often people use energy to speak about work done, when power would be the relevant term. Likewise, energy is often discussed only in terms of quantities. This leads to an unwarranted focus on concepts such as energy efficiency. Energy, however, consists of many important qualities. *Energy systems reflect the dynamics of various quantities of various qualities of energy.* Both the qualities and quantities of energy can, and should, be considered through design.

When the term energy alone is used in the context of energy systems, it is generally impossible to discern which quantities or qualities are at stake. Energy refers to the whole, but we generally need to speak intelligently about the parts and processes of energy systems. By way of analogy, it is a bit like stating that the sky has "color" when "blue" would more accurately describe the hue of the sky on many sunny days. To speak only of energy severely limits how we speak, and think, about energy. To be more explicit in this regard, reference to terms that reflect different qualities of energy are fundamental. The terms entropy, exergy, and emergy help articulate some of these important qualities of energy.

Entropy

Energy systems consist of energy that is available to do work and energy unavailable to do work, an extremely important qualitative difference. Again, all energy systems reflect varied quantities of varied qualities of energy. Available energy reflects the amount of work a system can perform. Unavailable energy can no longer be converted into work. This quantity is the entropy of the system. The energy in the universe is constant; what changes are the available and unavailable qualities of the energy in the system. Nicholas Georgescu-Roegen summarizes the topic of entropy well:

> entropy is an index of the relative amount of bound energy in an isolated structure or, more precisely, of how evenly the energy is distributed in such a structure. In other words, high entropy means a structure in which most or all energy is bound, and low entropy, a structure in which the opposite is true.[2]

The tendency of isolated systems to move towards equally distributed homogeneity – a state of maximum unavailable energy/maximum entropy – gives energy systems irreversible directionality: towards equilibrium. If the energy systems of architecture were isolated, then they would only tend toward maximal entropy. In non-isolated systems, however, the dissipation of available energy gradients is used to do work that reinforces the system and pushes it away from equilibrium. In this way, energy system design can be understood as the dynamic of systems towards and away from maximum entropy. Design and form are extremely important agents in this energetic, non-isolated dynamic of architecture.

Exergy

Whereas entropy refers to the quantity of unavailable energy in a system, exergy refers to the available energy in a system. Exergy is a measure of the maximum useful work possible before a system would enter equilibrium with its surroundings.

One very important and compelling aspect of exergy is that it is context-dependent. Exergy reflects the state of both the system and its surroundings. A bucket of 100°C water, for instance, in the Sahara Desert has far less exergy content than the same volume of water in the Arctic (Figure 1.7). Likewise, the solar radiation dissipated from the sun, a form of entropy, becomes the primary source of exergy on the planet Earth.

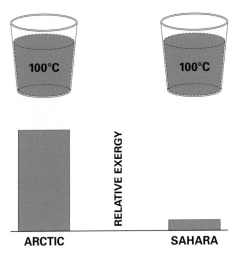

1.7 Exergy is context-dependent

As the system and the surroundings approach equilibrium, the exergy content approaches zero. As the system and the surroundings move far away from equilibrium, the exergy capacity increases. The energy systems in architecture operate away from equilibrium. In this regard, it is problematic to aim for a "zero energy" system design.

When people speak of energy efficiency, they most often have exergy efficiency in mind. Energy efficiency would be concerned with the efficiency of both available and unavailable energy in a system, a very confusing and misguided proposition. What matters in energy system design, however, is how work is done, at which rate and to what end.

Thus, in terms of thermodynamics and design, it is important to consider the **exergy matching** potential of a design. High quality energy should be used to do high quality work (Figure 1.8). Low quality energy should be used for low quality work. One astute aim of energy design, then, should be to match necessary work with appropriate qualities of energy, not just efficient quantities of energy. The concept of energy efficiency focuses only on the latter, not the former. As a result, those designs pay an overall energy penalty. "Focusing only on efficiency . . .," James Kay notes, "will lead to designs that use more exergy and produce more waste than they need to."[3]

In terms of exergy matching, it is useful to think of energy as a cascade of exergy: of high to low quality available energy. For example, electricity is a very high quality form of concentrated available energy. It can do many types of work – from illumination, to heating, to movement. However, from an exergy point of view that does not mean that electricity should be used for those myriad uses. It is a perversion, for example, to use electricity to heat a building. Heat is a relatively low quality form of work. Likewise, a 1000°F wood fire is not well exergy-matched for the purposes of warming a human body at 100°F (Figure 1.9). A better design would channel the dissipation of energy through a system, like a building, by matching various required uses with the correct quantity *and* quality of exergy. So, using electricity to move a body in a car is also an absurd exergy design, whereas a bicycle is better exergy matched for body movement.

While much energy design is preoccupied with exacting quantities, simply matching the magnitude of appropriate qualities (exergy) to the work required is generally a far more relevant concern. This at least focuses on the necessary work required of a process or design. This should be a first concern of energy design: Which orders of magnitude of exergy matter most for a given project?

Exergy, however, is only half of the problem for a non-isolated system design that consists of inputs, processes, and output as constitutive of its system and surroundings. There are other important system behaviors to consider as well. Thus, to complete an exacting understanding of energy systems, energy, entropy, and exergy alone are not sufficient. The concept of emergy helps complete our understanding of overall energy system structure, behavior, and design potential.

EXERGY MATCHING
ARCHITECTURE: HEAT A BODY

HOW TO EXERGY MATCH A BODY?

AIR

RADIANT

BOUNDARY LAYER

← **HIGH EMERGY/EXERGY RATIO LOW** →

HIGH EMERGY/EXERGY RATIO LOW

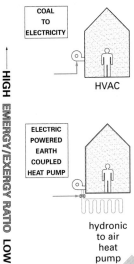

COAL TO ELECTRICITY

HVAC

electric radiant mat

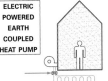

ELECTRIC POWERED EARTH COUPLED HEAT PUMP

hydronic to air heat pump

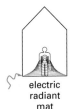

3 sided hydronic

wall boundary tempering

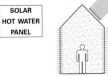

SOLAR HOT WATER PANEL

breathing wall with hydronics

6 sided hydronic activated surfaces

wall/body boundary layer tempering

1.8 Exergy matching: Thermal

EXERGY MATCHING
ARCHITECTURE: ELECTRIC LIGHT GALLERY (COAL SOURCE)

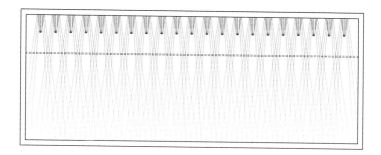

PATH DIAGRAM: 8 STEPS

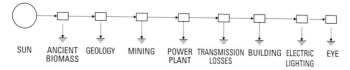

SUN   ANCIENT   GEOLOGY   MINING   POWER   TRANSMISSION   BUILDING   ELECTRIC   EYE
      BIOMASS   PLANT   LOSSES   LIGHTING

ENERGY TRANSFER

TRANSFORMITIES

1.9a Exergy matching: Lighting

EXERGY MATCHING
ARCHITECTURE: SAWTOOTH DAYLIGHT GALLERY

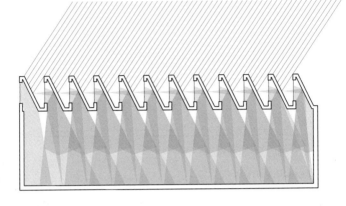

PATH DIAGRAM: 3 STEPS

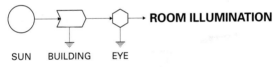

SUN   BUILDING   EYE

→ ROOM ILLUMINATION

ENERGY TRANSFER

TRANSFORMITIES

1.9b Exergy matching: Lighting

EXERGY MATCHING
(CLOSER TO BODY TEMPERATURE IS OPTIMAL)

1500°F
COMBUSTION
TEMPERATURE

150°F
WATER SUPPLY
TEMPERATURE
FOR AIR HEATER

95°F
SOLAR LOADED
BUILDING
SURFACES

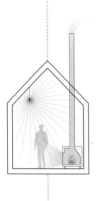

**COMBUSTION
+ LIGHT BULB**
(BIOMASS-BASED
ELECTRICITY & HEAT)

**CONVECTION
+ LIGHT BULB**
(PV-BASED
ELECTRICITY)

**INSOLATION
+ DAYLIGHT**
(SOLAR HEAT &
LIGHT)

HIGH
EMERGY YIELD
RATIO FOR BIOMASS
ELECTRICAL PLANTS

LOW
EMERGY YIELD
RATIO FOR PV
ELECTRICAL PLANTS

∞
EMERGY YIELD
RATIO FOR BIOMASS
ELECTRICAL PLANTS

EMERGY MATCHING
(HIGHER RATIO IS OPTIMAL)

1.10 Exergy matching: Architecture

Emergy

Emergy is perhaps the least familiar, and often least understood, energy concept. Yet it is one of the most comprehensive and revealing concepts. Whereas many who first encounter emergy as a concept presume that it must be a replacement for other forms of energy system analysis, it serves altogether different purposes and has different outcomes.

Emergy refers to the available energy, or exergy, of one form or another that is required, directly or indirectly, as an input for the production of product or service as an output. In other words, emergy reflects all the exergy captured and consumed in a process, from its origin to its present state. Emergy thus reflects both the historical record of total available energy used and, in so doing, reflects the relative capacity of a system component to affect the system: It is the total relative quality of its energy state. More than any other term described thus far, emergy has the farthest reaching capacities and effects.

Emergy is the most totalizing form of energy evaluation because, in terms of buildings and cities, it has the most complete system boundary. Whereas embodied energy analysis and lifecycle analysis exclude and externalize the bio-geophysical energy required to yield raw materials, emergy analysis includes these large and ecologically consequential formations of energy (see Chapter 3). Think about a forest around a lake in the Cascade Mountains. Do the square miles of surrounding trees require energy to grow? Does it take energy to evaporate water over the Pacific Ocean, lift the resulting vapor high in the atmosphere and then dump it into a dendritic system of streams that feed a lake? Does the lake contain potential energy and the river it feeds contain kinetic energy? Is energy required to convect whole tectonic plates? All of these bio-geophysical processes require energy and it is a grave thermodynamic and ecological error to presume, as other forms of energy analysis do, that these bio-geophysical resources are an infinite reserve of available forms of captured energy. Indeed, the notion that raw materials for building construction are plentiful and can be extracted at will for free from Earth's geobiosphere – and that these materials do not undergo any degradation or related deterioration in energy performance while in use – is alarming and entirely inaccurate. The flow of solar energy through these manifold bio-geophysical processes must further temper our understanding of the energy and materials that presuppose our buildings and cities.

A major, distinguishing advantage of emergy analysis is that it uses a single unit of measure, the solar emergy joule or emjoule. This allows for direct comparison of otherwise disparate processes and products. Since nearly all of the energy that drives terrestrial processes on Earth – about 98 percent – is based on incoming solar exergy, the solar emjoule is based on this solar exergy.[4] A unit of solar exergy by definition is 1. All objects and their associated processes – like bodies, buildings, and cities – are accumulations of emergy, as measured in the amount of captured and channeled solar energy required of the physical corpus and the work it accomplishes.

Since emergy is a record of cumulative energy quality required, it is an indicator of potential work and feedback. This cumulative accounting is recorded in terms of **transformities**. Transformity is the amount of emergy (in emjoules) required directly or indirectly to make a joule of energy of another type (Table 1.1). It thus reflects the ratio of required emergy input to available energy.

To comprehensively track the myriad types of energy and processes in a system – the salient task of emergy analysis – could be a daunting task for even the simplest of systems. Howard T. Odum had therefore derived a

Table 1.1 **Typical list of transformities (see Appendix for full list)**

Item		Solar Transformity		Reference Sources
		sej/g	sej/J	
Iron	Pig iron (w/ services)	2.83E+09	4.06E+06	Buranakarn, 1998, Table C-3
	Pig iron (w/o services)	2.65E+09	3.80E+06	Buranakarn, 1998, Table C-3
Lumber	Softwood	1.77E+09	4.40E+04	Updated in Buranakarn, 1998 (adapted from Haukoos, 1995, Table A-2a, p. 139–140); Odum, 1996, p. 308
	(w/ services)	8.79E+08	4.20E+04	Buranakarn, 1998, Table C-9
	(w/o services)	8.33E+08	3.98E+04	Buranakarn, 1998, Table C-9
	With plastic – HDPE (w/ services)	5.75E+09		Buranakarn, 1998, Table 3-12

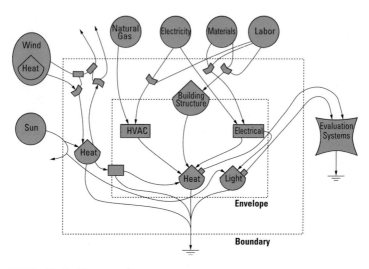

1.11 Simplified building system diagram

methodology for tracking the various inputs, processes, and outputs of any energy system. The flow of emjoules through a system is inventoried and illustrated in a **systems diagram** (Figure 1.11). The systems diagram records the various inputs, storages, pathways, processes and outputs of any given system. A central aspect of a systems diagram is the determination of a system boundary that distinguishes the system from its surroundings and the network of connections for energy flows.

The systems diagram indicates the hierarchy, relative magnitude, and direction of various energy flows. In emergy analysis, the convention is that the quantity of transformity increases from left to right. So, solar exergy – with a transformity of 1 by definition – is often an input located at the furthest left. These low quality but abundant forms of energy converge through system processes into fewer but higher quality forms of available energy. In terms of built environments, this convergence can be observed, studied, and designed. Energy that is no longer available to do work in the system is indicated as exiting the system through the bottom of the system diagram. Systems products are in the far right of a system diagram.

Each system diagram exists, however, at a particular scale and the series of indicated inputs and outputs must be understood as part of a much larger energy hierarchy. The primary purpose of emergy analysis is to grasp the relative position of a system component not just in terms of its role in a system but more generally in the universal energy hierarchy.

These energy system diagrams use a set of **symbols** to indicate various processes in the system (see Table 2.1). Together, the various flows, storages, and processes evident in a systems diagram indicate the energy hierarchy of a system. In other words, the systems diagram indicates the relative role of various systems components in relation to each other in terms of their emergy content. One use of emergy analysis, then, is to establish which components in the system might warrant greatest attention in terms of the feedback reinforcement for the system.

Feedback reinforcement

As will be discussed in greater detail in the next section of this chapter, the role of feedback reinforcement becomes very important in emergy system analysis and design (Figure 1.12). The processes and products on the right side of an energy system diagram reflect greater transformity and, therefore, greater capacity to affect the rest of the energy hierarchy. Powerful energy systems develop loops of "mutually enhancing interactions."[5] A common example is

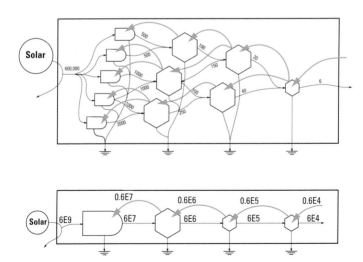

1.12 Feedback reinforcements in a system

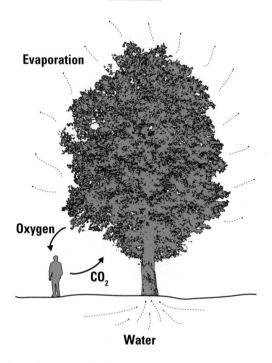

Evaporation

Oxygen

CO₂

Water

1.13 Feedback mutualities in an evolved system

the co-evolution of plants that intake the outputs of animals, both in terms of exhausted breath and night soils (Figure 1.13). A tree, for example, processes the "waste" of the animal and the animal processes the "waste" of the tree. It is the mutual interaction of the system that makes the energy system most powerful, not necessarily the efficiency of the plant or the animal alone. For these non-isolated systems, the system boundary must include these direct and indirect mutualities to understand the system at all.

Whereas most energy analysis is focused on the relative efficiency of a linear energy throughput in a system, emergy analysis adds the nuanced role of feedback for considering the power of the overall system. This importantly reflects the more non-linear behavior of energy systems. In this way, system design should make the overall system more powerful. It is not adequate to just make a system more or less efficient.

1.3 "Efficiency"

AS A TRANSITION INTO A DISCUSSION about the implications of the above energy systems concepts, structures, and behaviors, it is worthwhile to now consider the concept of "energy efficiency." Energy efficiency is perhaps the most common concept related to energy in the context of design. However, with the preceding vocabulary and set of concepts in mind, efficiency is not as simple a concept as it might initially seem. In many cases the concept distorts our understanding of energy systems.

For instance, as ecologist Sven Jørgensen notes, "[i]t is wrong to discuss an energy efficiency of an energy transfer, it will always be 100%."[6] As the first law of thermodynamics states, energy can neither be created nor destroyed. All energy is transferred, always, at full efficiency. While the idea of energy efficiency is thusly invalid, it is possible to think of exergy efficiency in this regard – the ratio of available energy consumption – but that already presupposes a different methodology and set of practices.

Further, it is difficult to discern what qualities and quantities are at stake in the concept of energy efficiency. Does the efficiency refer to available energy, or unavailable energy? The term simply lacks the specificity about energy system components, processes, and behaviors to reveal sufficiently relevant insight into a system design.

Even if energy efficiency was a valid aim, other problems persist. For example, James Kay observes that often "there is an underlying assumption that, if individual processes and subsystems are made efficient, then the overall system will be efficient. This assumption is only valid when the interconnections between elements of a system are strictly linear. This is rarely true in real physical systems."[7] It is important to note that energy systems, especially those away from equilibrium, require energy inputs and use just to keep the system far from equilibrium. To maximize the efficiency of the system, in common usage, reduces exergy content and drives the system towards equilibrium. This is not the goal of a non-isolated energy system design: quite the opposite.

This perhaps counter-intuitive observation points to the high degree of non-linearity in the energy systems of buildings. If energy systems were more linear, then perhaps energy efficiency would have greater efficacy. But energy systems are just that: a network of exchanges and feedbacks, none of which can be considered in isolation for long. Both the individual system and the overall behavior of the system are, together, most important to grasp. As Kay notes, at "any time one part of a system is optimized in isolation, another part will be moved farther from its optimum in order to accommodate the change. Generally, when a system is optimal, its components are themselves run in a suboptimal way. One cannot assume that imposing efficiency on every component in a system will lead to the most efficient system overall."[8]

Given these observations about energy systems, regarding building design Tim Allen concludes, "as the proper function of a building involves flux and energy degradation, putting minimization of energy dissipation at the top the list of priorities is at odds with full functionality of buildings."[9] Yet, despite these observations, the isolated foci of energy efficiency strategies remain ubiquitous in architecture and engineering.

One last observation related to the concept of energy efficiency helps shift attention to other, more important thermodynamic indicators of energy system design. Writing in 1955, long before the concept of energy efficiency was prevalent in design practice, Howard T. Odum and Richard Pinkerton observed that "systems perform at an optimum efficiency of maximum power output, which is always less than the maximum efficiency."[10] They emphasize that "natural systems tend to operate at that efficiency which produces a maximum power output."[11]

This more dynamic, systemic indicator of *maximum power* should be the focus of energy systems. The task of energy system design, then, is not the linear notion of energy efficiency but rather the relative power of the system. This forms an inordinately different, but often opposite, set of implications for energy in architecture.

1.4 The implications of energy, entropy, exergy, and emergy

THE FIRST SECTIONS OF THIS CHAPTER focused on the primary concepts and principles of energy systems. The remainder of this chapter will focus on the implications of energy systems for design and the relative power of the system. To fully grasp the implications of energy systems, it is finally important to understand certain universal propensities that emerge across all types, scales, and periods of energy systems. These propensities help orient design decisions and related policies. Design can and should emerge directly from these tendencies.

Maximum power

A primary tendency of energy systems is that systems that maximize power output tend to prevail in processes of self-organization. That is, the most powerful energy systems should be the aim of design. This insight into energy systems has evolved over the past century of thermodynamic observation. It has been successively articulated by a range of scientists in a number of adjacent fields. The history of this maximum power concept began with Ludwig Boltzmann. In his construal of the second law of thermodynamics as a probabilistic tendency, Boltzmann stated the following:

> The general struggle for existence of animate beings is therefore not a struggle for raw materials – these, for organism, are air, water, and soil, all abundantly available – not for energy, which exists in plenty in any body in the form of heat albeit unfortunately not transformable, but a struggle for entropy, which becomes available through the transition of energy from the hot sun to the cold earth.[12]

Building on evolutionary concepts from biology, Boltzmann discerned that life is not a struggle for matter or energy. Rather, he stated it is a struggle for entropy. In short, life is a struggle for extracting as much work as possible from available energy gradients before it is no longer available for work as entropy. Maximal entropy indicates the possibility of maximal extracted work.

Reflecting on Boltzmann, population dynamicist Alfred J. Lotka refined the above observation by stating,

> It has been pointed out by Boltzmann that the fundamental object of contention in the life-struggle, in the evolution of the organic world, is available energy. In accord with this observation is the principle that, in the struggle for existence, the advantage must go to those organisms whose energy-capturing devices are most efficient in directing available energy into channels favorable to the preservation of the species.[13]

Lotka's observation points towards not only maximal work and its resultant maximum entropy, like Boltzmann, but adds the consequential topic of feedback. Lotka's use of the term "efficient" should be understood in the context of efficiency discussed above: not maximal efficiency but most optimal efficiency for achieving, in this case, the goal of directing energy towards the preservation of the species. To this end, at no point should an energy system target low energy. As Lotka observes,

> In every instance considered, natural selection will so operate as to increase the total mass of the organic system, to increase the rate of circulation of matter through the system, and to increase the total energy flux through the system, so long as there is presented an unutilized residue of matter and available energy.[14]

In all cases, just as Boltzmann indicated that extracting maximal work is optimal, Lotka states that maximal material and energy flux is optimal as an indicator of maximum available potential. In non-isolated, far-from equilibrium cases, energy system tendencies are not oriented towards various minima; quite the opposite. Energy systems thrive on maximizing work and the rate of work, not minimizing energy consumption. Minimal energy consumption is neither the means nor the end of energy systems.

This propensity for maximum power was observed and systematically developed by systems ecologist Howard T. Odum. Based on Lotka's observations on the evolution of energetics, Odum stated that "during self-organization, system designs develop and prevail that maximize power intake, energy transformation, and those uses that reinforce production and efficiency."[15] By focusing on the maximization of power intake, the transformation of that energy, and its capacity to feedback, maximum power systems tend to prevail.

An important aspect of a maximum power system is not only its present state and dynamics but rather its dynamics over a long duration of time as well. Maximum power systems evolve over time by selecting more and more powerful organizations of matter and energy. Each system intakes more and more energy, transforms it in increasingly powerful ways, and learns to develop mutualities and feedback reinforcements, all in order to maximize the power of the system. So the temporal boundaries and evolution of a system are essential to consider.

Pulsing

Earlier in this chapter, we stated that – by accounting for all the energy required for a service or product – emergy expands not only the spatial considerations of energy analysis but also its temporal behavior as well. The state and behavior of any energy system are not constant but change over time. Odum observed that energy systems change in predictable, cyclical ways over time. He referred to this tendency as the "pulsing" of energy[16] (Figure 1.14).

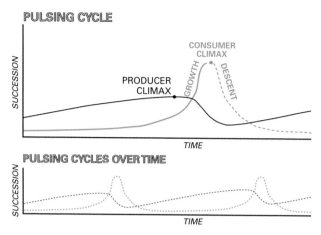

1.14 Pulsing cycles in energy systems

For energy systems to maintain maximum power over time, they cycle through periods of quick growth that evolve into more stable, diverse, and complex systems. A forest is a classic example. A forest begins with small flora – weedy structures in Odum's terms – that let onto larger shrubs and eventually to evolved forest ecologies. Each stage reflects an increasing level of emergy. Human settlements, as energy systems, evolve in similar ways. The architectural equivalent of "weedy structures" is replaced by more durable buildings and then perhaps more robust and diverse structures. Think about the evolution of Manhattan from early Anglo-American settlement to its present structure.

A durable system will evolve numerous non-linear mechanisms to continue the intake, transformation, and feedback of maximum power. However, to maintain maximum power, systems will often enter a radical downturn so as to complete and restart the pulsing of maximum power systems. The forest, again, is a prime example. A forest fire or wind event might catastrophically restart the uptake of the pulsing cycle. Likewise, the rise and fall of the Roman Empire exhibited similar system behavior over time.

Just as it is important not to externalize the spatial sources and inter-actions of a system and its surroundings, it is equally important not to externalize the temporal dynamics of energy system through analysis and design. Odum thus observes that "the ecological model of succession and climax has now been applied to national policy under the name sustainability. But seeking a constant level of civilization is a false ideal contrary to energy laws."[17] In this sense, a key component of energy system analysis and design has focused on the appropriate durability of energy system components. Here again, through its various spatial and temporal externalities, the energy efficiency of a building is an inadequate indictor of energy system performance.

The tendency for systems to develop towards certain states has been stated in multiple ways. For Odum it was maximum power. For theoretical ecologist Robert Ulanowicz, systems exhibit a propensity towards "ascendency" or towards not just increased material and energetic organization but the informational ascent of the system as well.[18] For Adrian Bejan, a system will evolve "in such a way that it provides easier access to the imposed currents that flow through it."[19]

While these authors will quibble with the nuances of the optimal state in each statement, it is first important to grasp that systems are attracted to, have a tendency towards, certain optimal states. These states, regardless of their much related expressions by the above and similar authors, orient the directionality of energy systems. These states should thus also orient a design agenda for energy as well. One goal of design, in this regard, is to push a system towards these recurrent states and optimal system behaviors.

1.5 Conclusion

THE AIM OF THIS CHAPTER is to elucidate the primary terms, structure, and behavior of energy systems in all of their spatial and temporal dimensions. The chapter aims to serve as an encompassing introduction to energy systems for designers. Each of the terms and concepts introduced here deserves greater attention than provided in the space of a single chapter. To this end, the remainder of this book, and the selected sources provided, serve as a guide into greater energy system understanding. The annotated bibliography, in particular, provides multiple sources to augment this admittedly brief introduction to the constitution of a very rich thermodynamic universe. Since this book focuses on the under-represented role of emergy systems in architecture, the subsequent chapters specifically expand upon the means and methods of emergy through principles and their applications.

1.6 Summary questions and observations to consider

1   Think about the concepts of open, closed, and isolated thermodynamic systems. Have buildings been considered and designed more as open or isolated systems in modern architecture?

2   What is the relationship between the terms energy, exergy, and emergy?

3   What is exergy matching design?

4   Since emergy is the amount of exergy required for a process or a product, consider the role of emergy matching design.

5   When, and in what ways, is the concept of "energy efficiency" a thermodynamically cogent concept?

6   How can buildings make the system that presupposes their construction more powerful?

Notes

1   Howard T. Odum as quoted in Tilley, D.R., "Howard T. Odum's contribution of the laws of energy," *Ecological Modelling*, 178(1–2), 2004; pp. 121–125.

2   Georgescu-Roegen, N., *The Entropy Law and the Economic Process*, Cambridge, MA: Harvard University Press, 1999; p. 5.

3   Kay, J.J., "Complexity theory, exergy, and industrial ecology," in Charles J. Kilbert, Ja Sendzimir, and G. Bradley Guy, eds., *Construction Ecology: Nature as the Basis of Green Buildings*. London: Spon Press, 2002; p. 92.

4   Hermann, W., "Quantifying global exergy resources," *Energy*, 31, 2006; pp. 1685–1702.

5   Odum, H.T., *Environmental Accounting: Emergy and Environmental Decision Making*, New York: Wiley, 1996; p. 289.

6   Jørgensen, S.E., "The thermodynamic concept: Exergy," in Sven E. Jorgensen, ed., *Thermodynamics and Ecological Modeling*, Boca Raton, FL: Lewis Publishers, 2000; p. 156.

7   Kay, p. 93.

8   Ibid.

9   Allen, T.F.H., "Applying the principles of ecological emergence in building design and construction," in Charles J. Kilbert, Ja Sendzimir, and G. Bradley Guy, eds., *Construction Ecology: Nature as the Basis of Green Buildings*, London: Spon Press, 2002; p. 120.

10 Odum, H.T., and Pinkerton, R.C., "Time's speed regulator: The optimum efficiency for maximum power output in physical and biological systems," *American Scientist*, 43(2) (April), 1955; p. 332.

11 Ibid., p. 331.

12 Boltzmann, L., "The second law of thermodynamics," *Populäre Schriften, Essay* 3, *Address to a Formal Meeting of the Imperial Academy of Science, 29 May 1886,* reprinted in Ludwig Boltzmann, *Theoretical Physics and Philosophical Problems,* S.G. Brush, trans. Boston: Reidel, 1974; p. 24.

13 Lotka, A.J., "Contributions to the energetics of evolution." *Proceedings of the National Academy of Science,* 8(6), 1922; p. 147.

14 Ibid., p. 148.

15 Odum, H.T., "Self-organization and maximum empower," in C.A.S. Hall, ed., *Maximum Power: The Ideas and Applications of H.T. Odum,* Colorado University Press, 1995; p. 311.

16 Odum, *Environmental Accounting,* pp. 242–259.

17 Odum, H.T. *Environment Power and Society For the Twenty First Century: The Hierarchy of Energy,* Columbia University Press, 2007; p. 63.

18 Ulanowicz, R.E., *The Ascendant Perspective,* Columbia University Press, 1997.

19 Bejan, A., "Constructal-theory network of conducting paths for cooling a heat generating volume," *International Journal of Heat Mass Transfer,* 40, 1996; p. 815.

chapter 2

Emergy analysis methodology

THE FIRST CHAPTER OF THIS BOOK provided a primary understanding of the various concepts and principles related to energy systems. That introduction to emergy and the hierarchy of energy provides a sense of the sweeping, comprehensive view of energy system consideration in emergy analysis. In so doing, it demonstrates how emergy analysis fundamentally differs from other types of energy system analysis. This next section articulates the methodology for emergy analysis.

First, however, it is important to grasp what emergy analysis is intended, and not intended, to help illuminate regarding energy systems. It is NOT a wholesale replacement of extant energy methodologies. In the first sense, emergy analysis can be understood as a form of scale analysis. Designers would benefit immensely from identifying and then operating on the appropriate, most strategic order of magnitude possible for a project. Emergy analysis establishes this hierarchy of magnitudes and thus indicates what respective systems and components matter for a project, given their magnitude and relative power in a system.

In another sense, emergy analysis can be used to make comprehensively informed, intelligent choices between, say, one type of insulation and another. In other ways, the relative amount of available energy inherent to a building and its operation can be evaluated. In each case, rather than impossibly wholesale and continuous emergy evaluation of buildings or cities, the intent is to address precise questions and discern the most powerful strategy for that stage of design. So emergy evaluation presumes a necessary, motivating question that helps organize and guide the evaluation.

2.1 Procedure: System boundary

THE FIRST STEP OF EMERGY ANALYSIS is the determination of what the analysis is exactly intended to address. Is the analysis looking at a specific process (the manufacture of concrete, for instance), the analysis of an object (a building over a two-century period), or pulsing of a larger system (a forest or civilization succession model)? Addressing this question will help determine the second aspect of the analysis, which is the most consequential decision in the procedure: the system boundary selection and definition (Figure 2.1).

The second step involves stipulating the system boundary for the analysis. Again, in thermodynamic terms, the system boundary distinguishes between what is in a system and what surrounds it. But whereas architects routinely conceive of boundaries as objects, the boundary is best understood as a zone of exchange and is characterized by the dynamics of its exchange behaviors. Thus, boundary selection requires considerable thought about what boundary dynamics are most relevant, what spatial and temporal scales matter, what is included and externalized from the system, and thus what the analysis ultimately reveals about an energy system. It is important to grasp that the system boundary is completely open to specification and thus requires deliberate consideration.

As stated above, one way to consider emergy analysis is as a type of energetic scale analysis. A useful outcome of emergy analysis is to simply grasp the relative magnitude of various energetic components of a building or a city. For instance, it may be useful to understand the relative power, in orders of magnitude, of constructional versus operational energy requirements in emergetic terms. Such an analysis would help discern which systems or processes in a building's energy hierarchy merit greatest emergetic concern. Without such analysis, as is so common, building components and systems are unscientifically privileged over others. This common oversight yields inexplicable exergy expenditures both in terms of design and in the ecology of the building itself.

Some basic questions that can guide the selection of a boundary include:

What boundaries and boundary dynamics are most relevant?
Boundaries occur where systems and surroundings interact. This dynamic zone might be a spatial or temporal zone, but the key feature of the boundary

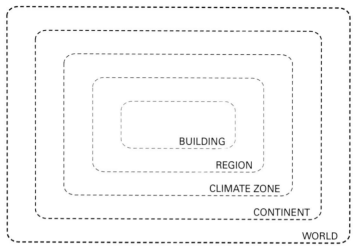

A BUILDING ON EARTH

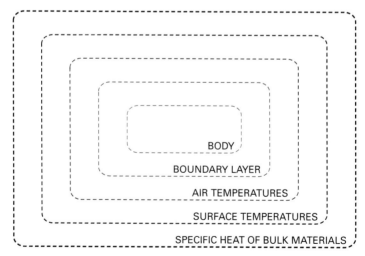

A BODY IN A ROOM

2.1a What is the proper system boundary for the energy system under consideration?

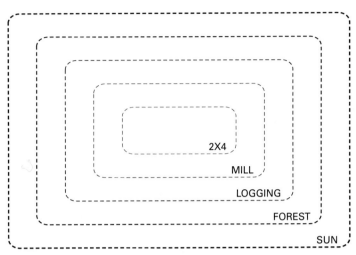

LUMBER

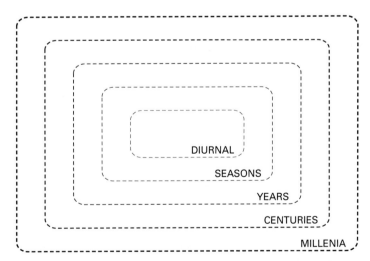

EVOLUTION OF CIVILIZATION

2.1b What is the proper system boundary for the energy system under consideration?

is the type and magnitude of matter and/or energy exchanging between the systems. It is the energetic exchanges that determine the boundary.

What spatial scale of analysis is relevant?

The thermodynamic, emergetic boundary of a building extends well beyond the physical perimeter of a building. Whether or not microclimatic dissipations of energy are immediately included as part of the building's energy system, or if the constitutive bio-geophysical emergetic sources of the building's materials are included as immediately part of the building's system boundary, each system boundary selection addresses fundamentally different questions, and outcomes, of analysis.

What temporal scale of analysis is relevant?

The thermodynamic, emergetic boundary of a building extends well beyond daily or annual considerations. Whether its anticipated life span is considered, or in the case of a building reuse, if the building's prior emergetic considerations are included, or if a building design fundamentally considers the role of durability and next-uses, again each of these temporal boundary conditions construes different system boundaries and different outcomes.

No matter what system boundary is selected – and one must be selected – the aim of the system boundary is to strategically discern what is, or what should be, included as part of the system under analysis. Once a reasonable hypothesis for the system boundary is determined, the next step in the emergy analysis procedure is the assembly of an energy system diagram (Figure 2.2). This will include all the inputs, outputs, components, processes, dissipation, and interactions in the energy system. Once all these system parameters have been identified, the components and processes can be assembled in an emergy evaluation table. Together, the energy system diagram and the emergy evaluation table are the core components of emergy analysis.

2.2 Procedure: Energy system diagram

AN ECOSYSTEM IS A COMPLEX interconnected system wherein both living and non-living networks operate together. Such networks exchange materials and energy, and, through feedback reinforcements, these networks self-organize through connectivity in space and time.[1] These energy flows, feedback systems, transformations, storages, and their complex interconnected ecosystems can be artfully represented with a symbol language – as developed in systems ecology – and referred to as a systems diagram. A skillful emergy diagram cogently distills and illustrates all the material and energy exchanges in an ecosystem. However, as Odum and Odum noted, attempting to model all the minute details of complex real world systems only leads to confusion.[2] Rather, models must be developed on scales appropriate to human understanding. With this understanding, system boundaries can be drawn and all relevant energy flows in and out of these systems can be tracked.

The methodology for constructing an energy system diagram includes a few primary steps. In each step, emergy researchers use a common set of symbols as an energy systems language (Table 2.1). First, the system boundary, discussed above, is determined and drawn as a bounding condition. Second, the primary sources of energy and material for the system are identified and listed. Third, the primary components within the system must be identified and situated in relation to each other. Finally, the various processes of interaction, production, consumption, and flow in the system can be identified and described. Finally, the flow of unavailable energy as well as the output of the system is considered and drawn in the diagram.

As an initial diagram is composed, it is likely that it will be rather complex with its myriad non-linear relationships. As the diagram is refined by adjusting the system components and processes, the diagram will become more coherent. Certain processes and components might aggregate to simplify the system. For example, the bricks, concrete, wood, and glass of a building might be considered as separate components in one analysis but aggregated as the building in another analysis, depending on the question motivating the analysis. Judgment is required. This process of diagramming the system might also force reconsideration of the system boundary itself. All of these steps, refinements, and reconsiderations are necessary for grasping the system and its surroundings. Once this inventory of boundary, components, and processes is complete, the quantitative portion of the emergy analysis can begin. There are a few types of system diagrams to consider based on the scales of phenomena and the principles of matter and energy, as noted by Odum and Odum in their *Modeling for all Scales: An Introduction to System Simulation* book.[3]

Table 2.1 Energy system diagram symbols[4]

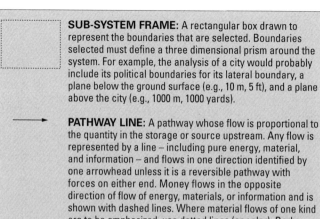

SUB-SYSTEM FRAME: A rectangular box drawn to represent the boundaries that are selected. Boundaries selected must define a three dimensional prism around the system. For example, the analysis of a city would probably include its political boundaries for its lateral boundary, a plane below the ground surface (e.g., 10 m, 5 ft), and a plane above the city (e.g., 1000 m, 1000 yards).

PATHWAY LINE: A pathway whose flow is proportional to the quantity in the storage or source upstream. Any flow is represented by a line – including pure energy, material, and information – and flows in one direction identified by one arrowhead unless it is a reversible pathway with forces on either end. Money flows in the opposite direction of flow of energy, materials, or information and is shown with dashed lines. Where material flows of one kind are to be emphasized, use dotted lines (or color). Barbs (arrowheads) on the pathways mean that the flow is driven from behind the flow (donor driven) without appreciable backforce from the next entity. Lines without barbs flow in proportion to the difference between two forces and may flow in either direction. Any outflow that still has available potential, materials more concentrated than the environment, or usable information is shown as a pathway from either of the three upper system borders, but not out the bottom. Pathways add their flows when they join or when they go into the same tank. No pathways should join or enter a common tank if they are of different type or transformity or are measured in different units. A pathway that branches represents a split of flow into two of the same type. [Suggested colors for pathways: Yellow – sun, heat flows, and used energy flows; Blue – circulating materials of the biosphere (water, air, nutrients); Green – producers, production; Red – consumers; Purple – money]

SOURCE: Any input that crosses into the boundary is a source: pure energy flows, materials, information, genes, and services. All of these inputs are given a circular symbol. Sources on the left side of the boundary relate to renewable sources (sun, wind, rain, geologic processes). The sources on the top right side follow a left-to-right order based on their solar transformity (say, natural gas comes before electricity through to human services. No source inflows are drawn into the lower side of the frame.

Table 2.1 **Energy system diagram symbols** – *continued*

HEAT SINK: Dispersion of potential energy into heat that accompanies all real transformation processes and storages; loss of potential energy from further use by the program. The "heat sink" symbol represents the dispersal of available energy (potential energy) into a degraded, used state, not capable of further work. Representing the second energy law, heat-sink pathways are required from every "transformation" symbol and every tank. At the start, one heat sink may be placed at the center bottom of the system frame. Then two lines at about 45° to the bottom frame border are drawn to collect heat-sink pathways. Using finer lines or yellow lines for heat sinks keeps these from dominating the diagram. No material, available energy, or usable information ever goes through heat sinks, only degraded energy.

STORAGE TANK: A compartment of energy storage within the system storing a quantity as the balance of inflows and outflows; a state variable. Any quantity stored within the system is given a "tank" symbol, including materials, pure energy (energy without accompanying material), money, assets, information, and image. Every flow in or out of a tank must be the same type of flow and measured in the same units. Sometimes a tank is shown overlapped by a symbol of which it is part.

ADDING PATHWAYS: Pathways add their flows when they join or when they go into the same tank. No pathways should join or enter a common tank if they are of different type or transformity or are measured in different units. A pathway that branches represents a split of flow into two of the same type.

INTERACTION: Two or more flows that are different and both required for a process are connected to an "interaction" symbol. The flows to an interaction are drawn to the symbol from left to right in order of their transformity, with the lowest-quality one connecting to the notched left margin. The highest transformity inflow, connected to the top of interaction symbol, acts as a feedback system. The output of an interaction is an output of a production process, a flow of product. These should usually go to the right, since production is a quality-increasing transformation.

Table 2.1 Energy system diagram symbols – *continued*

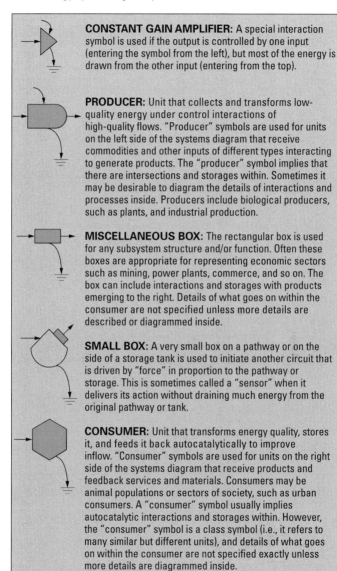

CONSTANT GAIN AMPLIFIER: A special interaction symbol is used if the output is controlled by one input (entering the symbol from the left), but most of the energy is drawn from the other input (entering from the top).

PRODUCER: Unit that collects and transforms low-quality energy under control interactions of high-quality flows. "Producer" symbols are used for units on the left side of the systems diagram that receive commodities and other inputs of different types interacting to generate products. The "producer" symbol implies that there are intersections and storages within. Sometimes it may be desirable to diagram the details of interactions and processes inside. Producers include biological producers, such as plants, and industrial production.

MISCELLANEOUS BOX: The rectangular box is used for any subsystem structure and/or function. Often these boxes are appropriate for representing economic sectors such as mining, power plants, commerce, and so on. The box can include interactions and storages with products emerging to the right. Details of what goes on within the consumer are not specified unless more details are described or diagrammed inside.

SMALL BOX: A very small box on a pathway or on the side of a storage tank is used to initiate another circuit that is driven by "force" in proportion to the pathway or storage. This is sometimes called a "sensor" when it delivers its action without draining much energy from the original pathway or tank.

CONSUMER: Unit that transforms energy quality, stores it, and feeds it back autocatalytically to improve inflow. "Consumer" symbols are used for units on the right side of the systems diagram that receive products and feedback services and materials. Consumers may be animal populations or sectors of society, such as urban consumers. A "consumer" symbol usually implies autocatalytic interactions and storages within. However, the "consumer" symbol is a class symbol (i.e., it refers to many similar but different units), and details of what goes on within the consumer are not specified exactly unless more details are diagrammed inside.

Table 2.1 **Energy system diagram symbols** – *continued*

AUTOCATALYTIC FEEDBACK: A unit that delivers an output in proportion to the input but is changed by a constant factor as long as the energy source is sufficient. High-quality outputs from consumers, such as information, controls, and scarce materials, are fed back from right to left in the diagram. Feedbacks from right to left represent a diverging loss of concentration, the service usually being spread out to a larger area. These flows should be drawn with a counterclockwise pathway (up, around, and above the originating symbol, not under the symbol). These drawing procedures are not only conventions that prevent excess line crossing and make one person's diagrams the same as another's, but they make the diagrams a way of representing energy hierarchies.

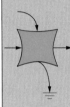

SWITCH: A symbol that indicates one or more switching actions. The concave-sided box represents switching processes, those that turn on and off. The flows that are controlled enter and leave from the sides. The pathways that control the switches are drawn entering from above to the top of the symbol. This includes thresholds and other information. Switching occurs in natural processes as well as with human controls. Examples are earthquakes, reproductive actions, and water overflows of a riverbank.

EXCHANGE TRANSACTION: A unit that indicates a sale of goods or services (solid line) in exchange for payment of money (dashed line). Price is shown as an external source. Where quantities in one flow are exchanged for those of another, the "transaction" symbol is used. Most often the exchange is a flow of commodities, goods, or services exchanged for money (drawn with dashed lines). Often the price that relates one flow to the other is an outside source of action representing world markets; it is shown with a pathway coming from above to the top of the symbol.

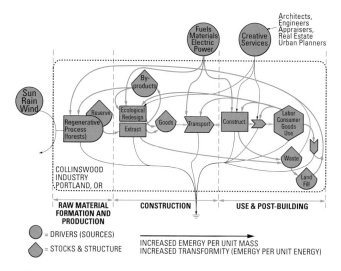

2.2 Building life cycle stages for emergy evaluation (adapted from Odum, 2002)

Figure 2.2 shows Odum's diagram of the Collinswood pine industry of Portland, Oregon, adapted for buildings.[5] The building life cycle stages, namely Raw Material Formation, Product, Construction, Use and Post-Building, are mapped to this systems diagram, which comprises both renewable and non-renewable energy and resource inputs at the broadest viewpoint. Each of the stages is represented by subsystem frame symbols within which energy flows, transformations, and storages occur. Used, degraded energy exits the subsystems, transformations, and storages via the heat sink (represented with an arrowhead).

Figure 2.3 shows the aggregated energy and material flows of the building structure from construction to post-building, where R represents renewable inputs, N represents the local non-renewable resources, and Fn and Fr represent purchased non-renewable and renewable inputs, respectively. The interaction symbol represents the production process of the building structure. It is to be noted that this production process extends to the entire lifetime of the building including maintenance and replacements whenever necessary.

The inputs for this production process include R, N, Fn, and Fr. Additionally, the reuse and reprocessing of the building structure during maintenance and replacement also becomes an input to this process. The building structure, represented as a storage symbol, feeds back actions to initiate the

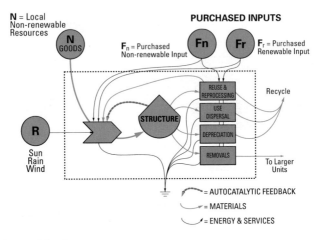

2.3 Aggregated flow diagram

production process, referred to as the autocatalytic feedback. For example, the need to maintain a structure, owing to material depreciation, acts as an initiating factor for the production of a feedback system. For the structure, there are four processes, namely reuse and reprocessing of materials; use dispersal; depreciation; and removals. While the reuse and reprocessing phase leads to production, the use dispersal and depreciation processes are recycled to disperse materials that return to background concentrations. Landfilled materials are considered a form of use dispersal. The removals process extends to larger units. Three types of pathway exist at this scale, namely autocatalytic, materials, and energy & services, as depicted in Figure 2.3.

Through the diagramming of energy systems, the various renewable and non-renewable sources and pathways at the building level can be understood. Figure 2.4 represents a typical building's energy systems diagram. While the renewable sources are organized on the left side, the inputs from the economy are shown on the top right side of the environmental window. The renewable inputs include sun, wind, rain, and geologic processes. The inputs from economy include water, natural gas, electricity, materials, and services. The building structure, represented as storage along with interior storage, encompasses the other building systems such as domestic water, heating, ventilation and air conditioning (HVAC), electrics, etc. The inner dashed line represents the building envelope through which heat and mass transfer happens. Take, for

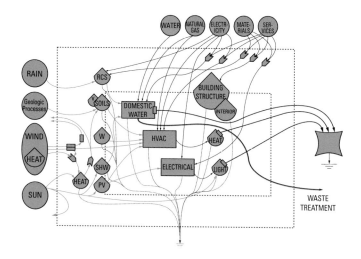

2.4 Systems diagram of a typical building

example, the renewable energy source of the sun. Daylighting is a form of energy that helps remove the necessity of electrical energy used for indoor lighting purposes.[6] Daylighting and electrical energy used for lighting purposes are two different types of energy, one renewable and the other which may be generated from renewable systems or non-renewables, and they additionally can act as substitutes for each other.

On-site renewable energy systems can be represented in the building diagram:

■ Solar photovoltaics: A photovoltaic system installed on top of the roof can be represented as storage, "PV," overlapping the building window (inner dashed line) with inputs from sun and outputs to electrical and HVAC processes.

■ Solar hot water systems: Similar to photovoltaic systems, a solar hot water heater system, "SHW," installed on the roof will have inputs from the sun and outputs to the domestic hot water system. This is assuming that there is no power requirement for pumping water to / from the system.

■ Wind power system: A wind power system, "W," will have inputs from wind source and outputs to electrical and HVAC systems.

However, if the system is not installed on the building, i.e., roof or building surface, then these storages can be moved away from the building storage symbol, i.e. between the environmental (outer dashed line) and the building (inner dashed line) windows. Besides, several other integrated systems can also be represented in the whole building diagram:

- Green roof and vegetation: Green roofs composed of soil and vegetation can be represented as storages, "SOILS" and "V," overlapping the building window. Inputs to these systems include the sun's heat, the wind's heat and air streams that nourish the soil and vegetation. The green roof's impact is shown by a link to the HVAC symbol directly, i.e. the reduction in energy used for conditioning the building.
- Rainwater collection system: This system can be presented as storage, "RCS," situated between the environmental and building windows with inputs from rain and other purchased inputs from the economy. The output is its interaction with the domestic hot water system.

Among other considerations, the use of energy and water is important. Operational energy use in the form of natural gas (to produce steam) and electricity (used for building systems such as HVAC, electrics, etc., and to produce chilled water), and operational potable water use can be appropriately identified in an emergy diagram. Energy used for building lighting, conditioning, etc., gets dispersed to background concentrations only to be reconstituted to form raw materials at a later time. In the case of wastewater generated at the building level, the energy used for wastewater treatment process can also be tracked.

2.3 Procedure: Energy system organization

THE INVENTORIED LIST OF COMPONENTS, processes and the flow between them, combined with the system symbol language, constitute the energy system diagram. The symbols in the diagram are organized by increasing transformities, from left to right. By definition, solar energy inputs, for example, would always be on the far left since the transformity of solar energy is 1. Information and human services would be placed on the far right due to the high order of magnitude of their transformity. Degraded energy from any process or transformation of energy is directed to the bottom center of the systems diagram. To develop a valid systems diagram, it is useful to consider the building as a series of linked spatial and temporal stages and states:

Raw material formation stage: Energy flows for raw material formation (represented by a circular external source of inflow symbol) cycle through bio-geophysical pathways – such as wind, rain, geological cycles – through inter-actions that range in duration from mere seconds to durations of millions of years. These bio-geophysical processes transform low energy concentrations into raw materials for primary building materials' manufacturing. For example, a tree requires energy to grow. It should be impossible to exclude and externalize these raw material formation energies in any form of energy analysis (yet that is the case in all but emergy analysis).

Product stage: The transformation of raw materials to primary building materials (products) requires three integrative transformations, namely raw material supply, via extraction, processing, etc.; the transportation of the aforementioned raw materials as represented by interaction, production symbols; and the manufacturing of the final product. These transformations use energy, water, materials, machinery, and labor.

Construction stage: The construction transformation process (represented by interaction, production symbols) uses energy, water, materials and machinery, and labor to construct the building structure (represented by a storage symbol). The structure gains heat from the sun directly and so does the construction transformation process; for example the setting of cement / concrete requires a certain amount of ambient temperature, etc., which is represented as solar irradiation.

Use stage: Building structures (represented by a storage symbol) undergo periodic maintenance that includes repair, replacement, and refurbishment owing to material degradation. Buildings require operational energy and water to operate HVAC, service hot water, and for electrical and lighting systems (represented by miscellaneous box symbol). Since, except for maintenance, the building structure remains intact for the duration of its useful life, the structure (represented by storage symbol) is common to both construction and use stages of the building life cycle. The operational energy used during the useful life of the building is diluted and dispersed back into the environment. Water used in the building is converted to wastewater which is processed directly on-site or distributed to wastewater treatment plants for further processing prior to disposal, which can create a decentralized pathway for possible productive reuse. Considerations regarding energy generated by renewable energy systems and their emergy content are included in this phase of the diagram as well.

While the operational energy use phase relates to energy consumption – for example electricity, chilled water, steam, natural gas, etc. – used during the useful life of the building, the maintenance phase covers all actions for maintaining the product or the building, as a functional whole, during its useful life. The other phases in the use stage are repair (covering all actions for maintaining through repair works for continued usage during useful life), replacement (covering all actions for replacing the product at the end of the product's service life), and refurbishment (covering all actions for restoring the product in a building to its former good condition); operational water use (which covers all potable and non-potable water use over the building's service life); and operational wastewater treatment.

End-of-life stage: In the context of emergy, after the useful life of a material in a building, two distinct pathways emerge, namely material recycle and dispersed material.[7] On one hand, in the material recycle pathway the material has a concentration that is distinguishable from the background concentrations. Although the material may have lost some energy used in "em-formation," – emergy required in changing the form of a material – it still possesses available energy that can be used as inputs for manufacturing of building materials. Take, for example, the Construction and Demolition (C&D) waste such as concrete which can be crushed and used to replace aggregate in concrete production. In emergy evaluation, the recycled material will take the value it replaces. In this case, the recycled crushed concrete, if used as an input in concrete production, will take the emergy value of the aggregate it replaces. On the other hand, in the dispersed recycle pathway, the material flows are dispersed to background concentrations that may have little or no available energy. In the case of the operational energy used for HVAC (thermal comfort), the energy disperses into the atmosphere through the building structure and re-enters the bio-geochemical cycle at a lowest energy state. Similarly, used-up materials must be transported to landfills. In this case, the materials still have distinguishable energy concentrations from their surroundings and flow into the dispersed recycle pathway, wherein the disintegration of their form and structure takes course over several million years forward through bio-geochemical cycles for formation as raw materials again.

After the useful stages of building, the building is deconstructed or demolished, the materials are collected and separated (represented by interaction, production symbols). This production of construction and demolition waste transformation process uses energy, water, materials, machinery, and labor. The processed material (represented by a storage symbol) is directed either to a landfill, a dispersed recycle pathway, or direct material reuse.

2.4 Procedure: Emergy evaluation table

ONCE THE ENERGY SYSTEM DIAGRAM is complete, the next step is the emergy evaluation table. After Table 2.2 is complete, emergy quantities are often added back to some energy system diagrams as the last step in the energy system diagram process (Figure 2.4).

The emergy evaluation table is a list of system components organized in rows. The columns of the table will include a range of values necessary for emergy evaluation. For example, in the evaluation of a building, this table would include a list of building materials as well as their quantities. A unit emergy value – such as the transformity (sej/J), specific emergy (sej/g), or emergy per monetary unit for each material (sej/$) – would be added in the next column, recorded as emergy per unit. The transformity for materials is the amount of emergy per unit of available energy (exergy). Specific emergy is the unit emergy value of dry matter mass (sej/g). The emergy per monetary unit (sej/$) relates emergy and money value systems. Each of these unit emergy values can be found in established emergy tables and databases, including the tables located in the Appendix of this book. The product of the material quantity and its listed transformity is the total solar emergy (sej), which can be expressed for the entire building lifetime as shown in Table 2.2.

Table 2.2 **Emergy evaluation table**

Source note	Items	Data (units/yr)	Unit	Solar emergy (sej/building lifetime)
RENEWABLE INPUTS (R)				
1	Sunlight	4.08E+13	J	3.06E+15
2	Rain (chemical potential)	1.82E+10	J	2.47E+16
3	Wind (kinetic energy)	1.63E+11	J	1.79E+16
	Total Renewable Inputs (R)			**4.57E+16**
NON-RENEWABLE STORAGES USED (N)				
4	Net topsoil loss	3.11E+07	J	2.89E+14
	Total Non-Renewable Storages Used			**2.89E+14**
PURCHASED INPUTS (F)				
5	Electricity	1.64E+12	J	5.11E+18
6	Chilled water	4.03E+12	J	1.21E+19
7	Steam	7.85E+11	J	2.88E+18
8	Water	7.24E+09	J	1.42E+16
9	Material Transport	2.48E+03	gal	1.63E+08
10	Construction Materials (except PV system)	1.80E+10	g	7.32E+19
11	Construction Materials (PV system)	1.31E+01	m²	8.38E+15
12	Construction Materials: Maintenance and Replacements (except PV system)	1.37E+09	g	4.53E+18
13	Construction Materials: Maintenance and Replacements (PV system)	2.62E+01	m²	1.68E+16
14	Construction Activities			3.69E+18
	Total Purchased Inputs			**1.02E+20**

2.5 Procedure: Emergy analysis

UNLIKE MANY FORMS OF ENERGY ANALYSIS, wherein the goal is a linear process of minimizing or optimizing consumption, emergy analysis of open thermodynamic systems is inherently more non-linear. As such, the linear minimization of energy flux is not a valid indicator of system power or efficacy. The central concern should be the relative power of the system. A powerful non-isolated system, again, may consist of many inefficient components. Often those components will be essential to driving the system towards more powerful aggregate behavior.

Unlike many types of energy system analysis, the purpose of emergy analysis is to evaluate the difficult whole of the energy system. This inevitably requires patience and a long view on energy system dynamics, but it is the most comprehensive and totalizing process for considering the role, and potential, of energy systems in architecture. The process will undoubtedly be new to many people, particularly designers, but engaging emergy analysis is an excellent way to begin to even imagine the profound non-linear dynamics that are inherent in the energy systems of architecture and urbanization. Thereby, it also begins to demonstrate the role of design in the energy hierarchies and energy dynamics of the universe.

Once the emergy values for systems, processes, and components has been established in the system diagram and evaluation table, a range of ratio indicators – elaborated in the next section of this chapter – are used to further evaluate the efficacy of the system. These thermodynamic indicators provide the most insight on the system as a whole.

For instance, the renewable and non-renewable emergy, both local and purchased, can be tracked (Table 2.3). Essentially, the energy inflow I = R+N, while the yield Y (outflow) = R+N+F. Using these inflows and outflows, the system can be assessed using ratios and properties.

Table 2.3 **Energy inflows and outflow**

R	The renewable flows (R) are: (i) flow limited (we cannot increase the rate at which they flow through the system); (ii) free (they are available at no cost); (iii) locally available.
N	The non-renewable flows from within (N) are: (i) stock limited (we can increase the rate of withdrawal, but the total available amount is finite in the timescale of the system); (ii) not always free (sometimes a cost is paid for their exploitation); (iii) locally available.
F	The feedback flows (F) may be: (i) stock limited (as above); (ii) never free; (iii) never locally available, always imported. **F = Fr + Fn**

Emergy ratios

Among others, there are five ratios that need to be addressed during emergy evaluation (Table 2.4). These ratios enable us to evaluate the characteristics of the system under investigation including the built environment, or its individual components. For example, these ratios can be studied at a whole building- or component-level. An example of component level assessment is the study of photovoltaic or rainwater collection or solar thermal systems independently of others.

Besides emergy systems diagramming and preparing the evaluation table, the heart of emergy analysis rests in the application of emergy ratios and results interpretation. The importance of emergy ratios cannot be overstated. Given several choices of building components and design alternatives, one can determine the optimal solution using these ratios as discussed below.

Ulgiati and Brown[8] provided a simple example to discuss the same. Consider three systems and, for the purposes of this book, assume that each system represents three design / material choices. Using a simple table (Table 2.5), the emergy values can be aggregated into R, N, F, and their total for each system. In this example, the total emergy (R+N+F) is maintained as 80 sej. Systems 2 and 3 have the same purchased energy (F); however, there are two subtle differences: (1) system 3 possesses more locally available renewables and (2) system 2 has higher locally available non-renewables. Similarly, systems 1 and 2 possess the same R and they differ in N and F. To elaborate, system 2 has higher N compared with system 1, and system 2 has lower F than system 1. The next step is to populate the emergy ratios table (Table 2.6) using the aggregated emergy values.

System 3 is the best choice, with the highest emergy sustainability index (ESI) (0.7) when compared with systems 1 and 2. ESI is the measure of the overall sustainability of the system as evident in system 3, which has low F, low N, and high R. That said, one can identify which of the two systems, 1 and 2, is better using the other emergy ratios. With the same percentage renewability (REN) for both systems, system 2 has high emergy yield ration (EYR), indicating that system 2 is better than system 1. In terms of aggregated emergy values, system 2 has high N and low F when compared to system 1. Although this approach helps us identify the best systems, in emergy terms, one needs to exercise caution when using the ratios, particularly EYR. EYR does not always mean a better choice, differs from case to case, and should be studied.[9]

Table 2.4 List of emergy ratios

Renewability (%REN)	Renewability provides a direct assessment of renewable energy source that was used up in the built environment. Lowering the purchased inputs will improve the building renewability. A good example is the use of renewable energy systems to reduce the power requirement, i.e., going off-grid. However, owing to the enormous amount of energy used in the manufacture of these renewable energy systems, there are instances when adding such systems may not improve renewability. However, the use of the sun's energy (renewable source) to both heat and light the indoor spaces will reduce electricity use (purchased input). Similarly, the use of rainwater (renewable source) for other non-potable uses will reduce water use (purchased input). $$\%REN = (R + Fr)/Y$$ Design objective: **High %REN**
Emergy Investment Ratio (EIR)	Emergy Investment Ratio measures the investment of the local environment, both renewable and non-renewable sources, in comparison with purchased inputs from the economy. $$EIR = Fn/(R + Fr + N)$$ Design objective: **Low EIR**
Emergy Yield Ratio (EYR)	Emergy Yield Ratio assesses the efficiency of the feedback from the economy to exploit the local resources, both renewable and non-renewable. If the building relies only on purchased inputs and less on local renewable and non-renewable sources, it is not healthy to the economy and the environment. On the other hand, through maximizing renewable resource use, the building's reliance on purchased inputs such as natural gas, electricity, water, etc., will be less. $$EYR = Y/Fn$$ Design objective: **High EYR**

Table 2.4 List of emergy ratios – *continued*

Environmental Loading Ratio (ELR)	Environmental Loading Ratio measures the investment of renewable source as a factor of all other inputs, both local non-renewable and purchased inputs from the economy. ELR may be used to evaluate alternatives of building components. $$ELR = (N + Fn)/(R + Fr)$$ Design objective: **Low ELR**
Emergy Sustainability Index (ESI)	Emergy Sustainability Index provides a measure of the overall sustainability of the system. **EYR/ELR** Design objective: **High ESI**

Table 2.5 Aggregated emergy evaluation table

	System 1	System 2	System 3
Locally renewable (R), sej	10	10	20
Locally non-renewable (N), sej	20	30	20
Imported from outside (F), sej	50	40	40
Total emergy used, sej	**80**	**80**	**80**

Table 2.6 Emergy ratios

	System 1	System 2	System 3
% Renew	0.12	0.12	0.25
EYR	1.6	2.0	2.0
ELR	7.0	7.0	3.0
ESI	0.2	0.3	0.7

Emergy space / occupant-intensive properties

Finally, particularly for buildings, there are two intensive properties that are relevant to emergy analysis:

■   Emergy density, a space-intensive property with unit sej/cubic m;
■   Emergy intensity, an occupant-intensive property with unit sej/person.

These two properties can be used to compare building alternatives: the lower the density or intensity, the better for the environment.

2.6 Emergy method exercise

AT THE CONCLUSION OF THIS CHAPTER, it may be useful to attempt a simplified emergy analysis. To work through the process, calculate the emergy of this solid wood building in Colorado. This wood building in Colorado has no mechanical systems, plumbing systems, or electrical systems. In that way, it provides a more direct focus on the materials of construction.

The first step in the emergy analysis process is to determine the volume of building material, then determine the total weight of material. In this case, the building was built using Standard Units, although the emergy calculations will be completed in metric units. The building requires 821.33 cubic feet of softwood timbers, 52.75 cubic feet of softwood flooring, and 36.09 cubic feet of softwood lumber. It has 21.25 cubic feet of plywood. The foundations include 128 cubic feet of concrete and 0.53 cubic feet of steel rebar. There is 5.62 cubic feet of glass and 4.34 cubic feet of rubber roof membrane. Outside of the steel rebar, there is 20.52 cubic feet of steel in the building.

Given these material quantities, you will need to find the total weight of the materials and then determine the emergy of the building with and without services using the compilation of emergy values in the Appendix of this book and the chart below as a guide. (The solution can be found in the Appendix – Table 8.2.)

2.5a Solid wood building in Colorado

2.5b Solid wood building in Colorado

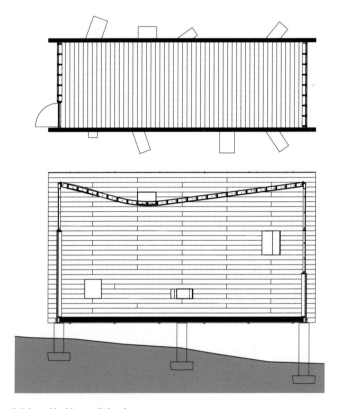

2.5c Solid wood building in Colorado

Table 2.7 Emergy evaluation table for Colorado mountain building

Colorado Mountain Building	Total Mass (g)	Specific Emergy (sej/g) w/ services	Specific Emergy (sej/g) w/o services	Emergy (sej) w/ services	Emergy (sej) w/o services
Softwood					
Plywood					
Steel (BOF recycled)					
Concrete					
Glass (float)					
Roof membrane					

2.7 Summary questions and observations to consider

1   Given this emergy analysis, what systems in this building have the greatest capacity for system feedback?

2   How would this compare with a more conventional layered wall built with stick lumber, insulation, plywood, finish materials, and a rain screen?

3   How would modifying the system boundary of this exercise change its results?

Notes

1   Ulgiati, S. and Brown, M.T., "Emergy and ecosystem complexity," *Communications in Nonlinear Science and Numerical Simulation*, 14, 2009; pp. 310–321.

2   Odum, H.T., and Odum. E.C., *Modeling for All Scales, an Introduction to System Simulation*, San Diego, CA: Academic Press, 2000.

3   Odum and Odum, *Modeling for All Scales*.

4   Adapted from Table 1.2 and Appendix A from Howard T. Odum, *Environmental Accounting: Emergy and Environmental Decision Making*, New York: John Wiley & Sons, Inc., 1996; pp. 5, 290–293.

5   Drawn by author based on Howard T. Odum, "Material circulation, energy hierarchy, and building construction," in Charles J. Kilbert, Jan Sendzimir, and G. Bradley Guy, eds., *Construction Ecology: Nature as the Basis of Green Buildings*, London: Spon Press, 2002; p. 61, Figure 2.15.

6   Meek, C., and Wymelenberg, K., *Daylighting and Integrated Lighting Design*, London: Routledge, 2014.

7   Brown, M.T. "Areal empower density, unit emergy values, and emformation," in *Emergy Synthesis 3: Theory and Applications of the Emergy Methodology, Proceedings of the Third Biennial Emergy Conference*, Gainesville, FL, 2005.

8   Ulgiati, S., and Brown, M.T., "Monitoring patterns of sustainability in natural and man-made ecosystems," *Ecological Modelling*, 108, 1998; pp. 23–36.

9   Raugei, M., Bargigli, S., and Ulgiati, S., "Emergy yield ratio: Problems and misapplications," in *Proceedings of the Third Biennial Emergy Conference*, Gainesville, FL, 2005.

chapter 3

Comparing emergy analysis with life cycle assessment tools

THE GOALS OF THIS CHAPTER ARE THREEFOLD. First, this chapter will provide a detailed comparison of emergy analysis with current life cycle tools and methodologies. Second, it will provide a fundamental understanding of some of the inherent problems in current tools used for determining the sustainability of the built environment. Third, it will introduce a dynamic platform for involutionary integration of varied sustainability concepts for use by architects, engineers, and building operators alike.

The leading building rating systems in the United States, such as Green Globes[1] and LEED,[2] are similar to most of the other rating systems worldwide and use a point-based approach to assess the sustainability of a building. Recently, there is a strong push by rating systems to include Life Cycle Assessment (LCA) – in addition to typical operational energy use calculations[3] – by offering credits that can be accumulated to achieve higher certification levels. LCA is a compilation and evaluation of the inputs, outputs, and the potential environmental impacts of a product system throughout its life cycle.[4] The typical stages studied using LCA are product, construction, use, and end-of-life. The LCA tools compared in this chapter are sector-based tools (EIO-LCA) and process-based tools (Athena® Impact Estimator or IE); a hybrid-LCA tool known as BIRDS (Building Industry Reporting and Design for Sustainability); and a fully extended assessment method, Ecologically-based LCA (Eco-LCA). The primary differences among the tools are their system boundaries.

EIO-LCA and Athena® IE: For sector-based analysis, the U.S. Economic Input-Output (EIO) database uses aggregate industry sectors and relies on U.S. IO data. The most recent U.S. IO data available is for the year 2002, with 428 sectors. Carnegie Mellon's EIO-LCA software is widely used in the United States.[5] A sector-based approach offers an easy-to-use solution, and the system boundary for analysis is the entire economy of the country. This may render the approach useful for a whole building material and energy flow accounting.

In process-based analysis, a detailed tracking of each of the diverse processes within the system boundary is inventoried. This can be a lengthy procedure leading to high costs, time, and issues related to data confidentiality and verifiability. As previously mentioned, an example of process-based LCA is the Athena® IE.[6] Both sector- and process-based LCA approaches have drawbacks. Researchers have thus developed hybrid LCA approaches which combine these two approaches in order for them to complement and compensate for each other's strengths and weaknesses.

BIRDS: The hybrid-LCA approach uses initial embodied energy (sector-based method) with detailed accounting of processes (process-based method), which is then input into the sector-based model to assess specific actions. BIRDS uses a similar approach where it combines "top-down" environmental IO data and "bottom-up" process data to achieve a better estimate. In this tool, once the emissions are estimated, they are mapped such that specific impact categories – such as the impact per functional unit of product produced – are reported. Yet, one of the critical stages of product – the exergy required for raw material formation – is overlooked in all of these traditional LCA methods discussed above. In other words, the system boundary for these tools is too limited to understand the actual hierarchy of energy in buildings. For architects interested in the energy systems of buildings, this vast domain of energy should be difficult to externalize and dismiss from the system boundary of a building.

Eco-LCA: Eco-LCA can address energy use further upstream within the total building system by primarily relying on U.S. EIO data and emergy. Eco-LCA uses a 1997 IO database. The primary reason for a fully extended assessment is the inclusion of ecosystem goods and services into LCA for improved decision making during the design, construction, operation, and decommissioning of buildings in order to minimize negative environmental impact and to optimize the use of natural resources.

3.1 Comparison of emergy and life cycle tools

THIS SECTION WILL, in a concise and clear manner, identify and present the subtle differences and commonalities in the typically used life cycle tools. The underlying system boundaries, data inputs and outputs, and a detailed comparison of the tools are provided here. Most of the life cycle tools estimate environmental impact categories such as Global Warming Potential (GWP), Ozone Depleting Potential (ODP), etc., through aggregation of individual pollutants in the equivalent form for the said impact category.

System boundaries: For consistent system boundaries in these tools, four building life cycle stages are used: product, construction, use, and end-of-life. To recall, the product includes raw material extraction, transportation, and manufacturing of the product; the construction stage includes transportation of the finished product to the building site and any energy used up during construction/installation; the use stage is more comprehensive and includes maintenance (all actions for maintaining the product or the building as a whole during its useful life), repairs (replacing the product based on the need dictated by that product's service life), refurbishment (restoring the product to its former good condition), and operational energy use; the end-of-life stage comprises demolition, transportation, waste processing, disposal to landfill and reuse/recycle/recovery. Figure 3.1 maps the LCA tools and emergy analysis over the building life cycle stages. While EIO-LCA and Athena® IE cover all but raw material formation stages, the Eco-LCA and emergy tools extend to all building life cycle stages, including the energy required to grow a tree or other similar raw material formation energies.

Data inputs and outputs: Data collection and preparation is a necessary step prior to analysis. For inputs, data can be gathered from the bill of materials for a building, construction drawings, finish schedules, commissioning reports, operational energy and water use data from utility bills, and other resources such as reports submitted for building rating certification. Interior furniture, fixtures, and equipment – such as white boards, chairs, and projector screens – can be quantified and used as inputs in addition to building structure and envelope components. However, in the case of Athena® IE, the building material database is restricted to the structure and envelope systems that are

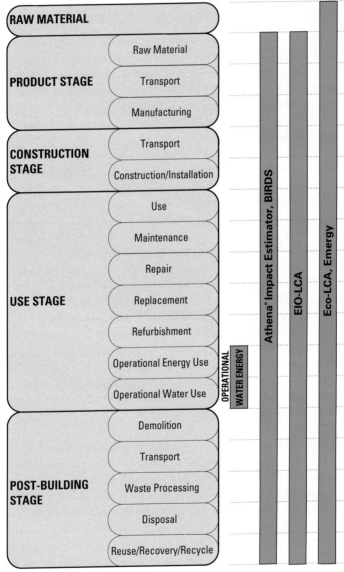

3.1 Emergy and LCA tools mapped on life cycle stages

Table 3.1 Emergy and LCA tools – inputs and outputs

Tool	Inputs	Outputs
		Available
Athena® Impact Estimator	• Location • Building Element Quantities	Energy use in TJ.
		Impact Categories: Primary Energy Consumption, Acidification Potential, GWP, HH Respiratory Effects Potential, ODP, Photochemical Smog Potential, Eutrophication Potential.
EIO-LCA	• US $ (inflation adjusted) • Sector ID	Conventional Air Pollutants: CO, NH_3, NOx, PM10, PM2.5, SO_2, VOC.
		Greenhouse Gases: CO_2e, CO_2 Fossil, CO_2 Processes, CH_4, N_2O, HGC/PFCs.
		Energy (in TJ).
		Toxic Releases: Total Air, Surface Water, Underground Water, Land, Off-site, etc.
		Water Withdrawals, Transportation (Air, Oil Pipe, Gas Pipe, Rail, Truck, Water, International Air, International Water), Land Use, Hazardous Waste Generation.
BIRDS	• Location • Building Types • # of Stories	Energy use in TJ.
		Impact Categories: Primary Energy Consumption, Acidification Potential, GWP, Human Health, Respiratory Effects Potential, ODP, Photochemical Smog Potential, Eutrophication Potential, Fossil Fuel Depletion, IAQ, Habitat Alteration, Water Intake, Criteria Air Pollutants, Ecological Toxicity.
Eco-LCA	• US $ (inflation adjusted) • Sector ID	Similar to EIO-LCA, plus, I+E Exergy (Ecological Cumulative Exergy Consumption or ECEC), I Exergy (Industrial Cumulative Exergy Consumption).
Emergy	• Building Element Mass • Solar Transformities • UEVs	EGS in sej; emergy indices.

most commonly used. Comparatively, since EIO-LCA and Eco-LCA are sector-based approaches, it is not limited to the components of the building that can be included in the analysis, as long as a particular material is covered under a specific industrial sector. Therefore, EIO-LCA and Eco-LCA can provide a more elaborate assessment (not necessarily accurate to a particular system), since components such as mechanical, electrical, and plumbing can be input into the analysis. For EIO-LCA and Eco-LCA methods, cost of materials is used as inputs after adjusting for inflation.

Athena® IE allows input of site location, which then can be used to generate primary fuel mixes of operational energy based on regional / local utility provider information. In the case of EIO-LCA and Eco-LCA, the operational energy use related to embodied energy is derived based on available sector data; for example, sector ID 221100 corresponds to power generation and supply. In essence, the energy uses are not measured in the same scale – one is measured at a regional scale using process-based data (Athena® IE) and the other is at a national scale using the producer price information to derive outputs (sector-based approach, EIO-LCA or Eco-LCA).

For outputs, emergy and Eco-LCA methods have some common intersection, for instance, the sej values from emergy and the Ecologically Cumulative Exergy Consumption (ECEC)-based sej values from Eco-LCA. In a typical LCA, depending on the outputs, the impact categories can be determined and combined together to estimate an environmental assessment score. Although there are several other outputs that are available for LCA methods such as emissions and impact categories, for the purposes of this book only the energy use in terajoules (TJ) (for all methods except emergy) and sej (for emergy and Eco-LCA) are compared. Using a case study building, Rinker Hall in the University of Florida campus, Chapter 5 of this book compares results from LCA tools and emergy analysis.

Beyond the traditional comparison of TJ and sej, there are a number of other outputs that can be used for effective communication of impacts. Take for example, the CO_2 emissions per year derived from EIO-LCA and Eco-LCA. Using this data, designers can estimate the amount of forested acres needed to sequester the carbon emitted. Similarly, the Disability-Adjusted Life Year (DALY), an overall disease burden due to emissions, can also be estimated from these outputs, i.e. this offers some additional intelligence to human health impacts due to emissions. In the case of Rinker Hall, assuming a 75-year service life, the number of forested acres of southern pine trees needed to sequester the

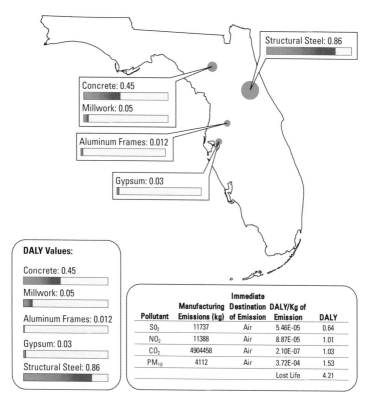

Structural Steel: 0.86

Concrete: 0.45

Millwork: 0.05

Aluminum Frames: 0.012

Gypsum: 0.03

DALY Values:

Concrete: 0.45

Millwork: 0.05

Aluminum Frames: 0.012

Gypsum: 0.03

Structural Steel: 0.86

Pollutant	Manufacturing Emissions (kg)	Immediate Destination of Emission	DALY/Kg of Emission	DALY
SO_2	11737	Air	5.46E-05	0.64
NO_2	11388	Air	8.87E-05	1.01
CO_2	4904458	Air	2.10E-07	1.03
PM_{10}	4112	Air	3.72E-04	1.53
			Lost Life	4.21

3.2 A mock-up showing DALY values overlaid on a Florida map to show the locations where some of the building materials and systems were manufactured (concrete, millwork, gypsum, structural steel, and aluminum frames)

CO_2 emissions and the DALY values are listed in Tables 3.2 and 3.3. Moreover, location-based DALY values for materials used in Rinker Hall are overlaid on the Florida map,[7] in Figure 3.2.

Characteristics of Emergy and LCA tools: In Table 3.4, the characteristics of emergy and LCA tools are discussed under seven categories: (1) type; (2) intuitiveness, user-friendliness (easy, medium, hard); (3) inputs of building components, particularly materials and assemblies, and interior components; (4) energy used in operations, particularly electricity and other energies, water,

Table 3.2 Forested acres of southern pine trees needed to sequester CO_2 emitted during Rinker Hall's fully extended service life

Rinker Hall Life Cycle Phase	Forested Acres Needed
Material Manufacturing, Construction, Transport of Materials to Job Site, Transport of Construction Waste	5.73
Operation	99
Material Replacement	1.7
Destruction/Demolition, Transport to Landfill/Recycling	0.26
Total	**166.69**

Table 3.3 DALY values for Rinker Hall by phases

Phase	DALY
Material manufacturing	4.21
Construction Phase	0.66
Transport of Materials to Job Site	0.0309
Transport of Construction Waste	0.0195
Operations	457
Maintenance	1.27
Deconstruction/Demolition	58
Transport to Landfill/Recycling	0.02
	521.21

Table 3.4 **Emergy and other LCA tools**

Categories	Sub-Categories	Athena® Impact Estimator	EIO-LCA
Type	Sector, Processed or Hybrid	Process-based LCA	Sector-based LCA
Intuitiveness, User-friendliness		Medium	Medium
Inputs – Building Components	Building Materials and Assemblies	Data is limited to materials for the building envelope and structure. Not all building materials and assemblies are available and may not represent actual design.	Data for EIO model is a good representation of manufacturing industry (steel, roofing material, paints, cement, etc). It is possible to represent actual design.
	Interior Building Components	Only building envelope and structure are included in the database. Electrical systems, mechanical equipment, finishes, etc., are not included.	It is possible to develop energy use for electrical systems, mechanical equipment, finishes, etc.
Operational Use	Electricity, Chilled Water, Natural Gas, Diesel, etc.	Yes	Yes, however, IO data does not correspond to actual primary energy used by the utility provider.
	Water	No	It is possible to estimate life cycle energy used in operational water consumption.
	Wastewater	No	It is possible to estimate life cycle energy (electricity and chemical) used in wastewater treatment. Emissions to air cannot be modeled.
Database	Database Source	No	Publicly available data.
	Database Issues	Athena® Impact Estimator uses process-based data acquired from both U.S. and Canadian industries. The transportation distances are maintained as a constant similar to other process-ID-based LCA tools such as GaBI and SimaPro.	EIO-LCA uses 2002 and 1997 US IO data. Several sector IDs exist for the same material. Professional expertise is required to select the appropriate sectors.
Outputs	Valuation of Ecosystem Services	No	No
	Indicators of Environmental Impact	Yes	It is possible to develop indicators of environmental impact.
	Geospatial Information	It is possible to develop geospatial information.	It is possible to develop geospatial information.
Uncertainty		Uncertainty inherent in process-based data.	Uncertainty inherent in original EIO model data.

Table 3.4 **Emergy and other LCA tools** – *continued*

BIRDS	Eco-LCA	Emergy
Hybrid-LCA	Sector-based LCA	Sector-based (to develop emergy transformity)
Easy	Medium	Medium
BIRDS uses 11 building proto-types and the data is limited to only construction types of these 11 building types. Therefore, actual design may not be represented in the tool.	Data for EIO model is a good representation of manufacturing industry (steel, roofing material, paints, cement, etc). It is possible to represent actual design.	Limited set of values to match with building materials. It is possible to represent actual design.
Electrical systems, mechanical equipment, finishes, etc., not included.	It is possible to develop energy use for electrical systems, mechanical equipment, finishes, etc.	It is possible to develop energy use for electrical systems, mechanical equipment, finishes, etc.
Tool estimates operational energy use based on the limited inputs. The emissions data relatesto the primary energy used by the utility provider.	Yes, however, IO data does not correspond to actual primary energy used by the utility provider.	Yes, however, limited emergy transformity data available for applying actual primary energy used by the utility provider.
No	It is possible to estimate life cycle energy used in operational water consumption.	It is possible to estimate life cycle energy used in operational water consumption.
No	It is possible to estimate life cycle energy (electricity and chemical) used in wastewater treatment. Emissions to air cannot be modeled.	It is possible to estimate life cycle energy (electricity and chemicals) used in wastewater treatment.
Publicly available data	Publicly available data	Publicly available data
BIRDS uses life cycle inventory data for 11 building prototypes and includes operational energy use data developed using detailed energy simulations. Significant updates are required for determining operational energy use data.	Eco-LCA uses 1997 U.S. IO data. Issues related to EIO-LCA sector IDs apply here. Besides, current version of Eco-LCA uses emergy transformities derived from different emergy baselines. Professional expertise is required to select the appropriate sector ID.	Several emergy transformities exist for the same material owing to different processes for material production. Professional expertise is required to select the appropriate transformity.
No	Yes	Yes
Yes	It is possible to develop indicators of environmental impact.	No
No	It is possible to develop geospatial information.	It is possible to develop geospatial information.
Uncertainty inherent in lifecycle inventory data and operational energy use estimation.	Uncertainty inherent in original EIO model data and emergy transformities used in the model.	Uncertainty in use of emergy conversion factors extracted from the literature.

and wastewater; (5) database specifics such as source and issues; (6) outputs in terms of valuation of ecosystem services, environmental impacts, and geospatial data; and (7) uncertainties. Table 3.4 lists the characteristics of emergy and LCA tools.

3.2 Balancing evolutionary growth through involutionary integration

In an attempt to balance the evolutionary growth of buildings, it is imperative to understand the inherent problems that exist in current tools and rating systems, namely:

- **Disparate and disintegrative systems**: Most energy analysis tools and methodologies do not include all "involved" elements in one integrative environmental accounting platform. As one takes a closer look at the tools discussed here, it is evident that most of the resources needed to elevate the sustainability of the building are easily within reach, yet disintegrated – largely due to the fact of the fragmented landscape of these advanced analysis tools.

- **Lack of ecologically derived benchmark**: There are benchmarks based on operational energy and water uses; however, there is a serious lack of accounting of ecosystem services and impacts to habitat / biodiversity and human health. Needless to say, there has not been a single attempt to benchmark built environments based on impacts to habitat / biodiversity and human health, or, simply put, *there is no ecologically derived benchmark for buildings*.

- **Lack of a coherent space–time context**: These tools and methodologies do not include the geography of the impacted areas, i.e. those areas that have taken the wrath of all the emissions and other impacts due to manufacturing of products used in buildings. In almost all scenarios, the emissions due to the manufacturing of building materials and the building site do not co-locate. Yet, most of the tools we use to estimate emissions do not make this distinction. Moreover, building materials emit over time, impacting Indoor Environmental Quality (IEQ) as well. This lack of consideration for the context of space and time can also affect intake fraction projections, which can skew otherwise accurate assessments of human health impacts.

■ **Lack of comprehensive assessment procedures**: These tools do not provide comprehensive assessment of all building components. Even if this is done, questions arise about the data of post-building scenarios, particularly energies related to demolition, waste processing, disposal, transportation, and reuse / recovery / recycling. This poses a major challenge to the analysis itself – whether the analysis still has any meaning at all, especially if we could not achieve tracking of all energies in the life cycle of materials used in the building.

■ **Increased focus on operational energy optimization**: Operational energy is only a portion of a building's life cycle flow, and the notion that if operational energy is curtailed to a bare minimum[8] the impacts related to the building will disappear is entirely inaccurate. For example, they either focus on energy or materials in terms of quantities but not their qualities, with emergy analysis as the only exception.

A critical component in the development of an integrated platform for energy considerations is the necessary analysis that identifies all involved material and energy flows from the formation of raw materials to end of life of the building. As the above analysis indicates, there is no dispute that environmental accounting of buildings is the best, most comprehensive approach to measure environmental impacts through direct accounting of resource costs, i.e. resource consumption and impacts over the entire life cycle of the building, from extraction to demolition and disposal.[9]

We acknowledge that the term "life cycle" is an anthropogenic conceit, one that skews our understanding of matter and energy. Building materials, for instance, do not have a life, are not alive, while the total energetic content of these materials far exceeds human engagement and use of that energy. This energy in matter was present in ecosystems long before humans strove to utilize it and shall remain long after humans are gone. Thus, the accounting of material energy beyond human use-value is an essential aspect of total environmental accounting such as emergy analysis. Energy dissipates, accumulates, and transforms, but it does not have a "life." It is better, in our mind, to simply acknowledge this dissipation and develop methods accordingly. Human-centric concepts and building-centric systems boundaries occlude important quantities and qualities of energy. Our accounting of the matter and energy in buildings should not suffer these externalizations.

As designers, our attempts to achieve the larger goal of buildings that aim for maximal productive environmental impact are akin to solving a jigsaw puzzle, in which emergy and LCA tools are part of the larger solution. Other pieces include assessments related to energy, water, land use, non-energy materials, transportation infrastructure, and more. Designing accordingly requires data sources from comprehensive assessment in one integrated platform. Furthermore, a necessary step towards achieving this goal of a truly sustainable building is for the hidden social, economic, and environmental costs of our design choices to be revealed. The Dynamic-SIM (Dynamic-Sustainability Information Modeling) platform under development at the University of Florida is an embodiment of this involutionary integration to balance evolutionary growth.[10] The substratum of this platform is the graphics environment that can be used for domain modeling, simulation, and visualization (see Figures 3.3 and 3.4).

3.3 Bird's eye view of UF Campus, Gainesville, in Dynamic-SIM Workbench. At present, historic energy use data is used, at building level. Energy data includes electricity, water, chilled water and steam, at monthly and annual level. Users can "fly" around buildings

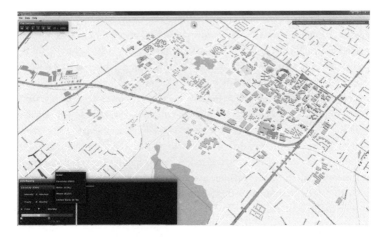

3.4 A "play" button enables maintenance engineers to visually evaluate energy use of buildings. A user interface allows data extraction and visualization seamlessly

3.3 Summary questions and observations to consider

1 Why is the present focus on operational energy optimization, alone, problematic?
2 What is an externality in the context of energy systems in architecture?
3 What is the system boundary of operational energy analysis versus life cycle analysis versus emergy analysis?
4 What does the DALY metric refer to?
5 What is the most totalizing metric for grasping the relative negative and positive impacts of buildings and their environments?

Notes

1 Green Globes for New Construction is a rating system developed and managed by the Green Building Institute (www.thegbi.org). This rating system is a variant of the UK rating system, the Building Research Establishment Environmental Assessment Methodology, also referred to as the BREEAM. Under the "Resources, Building Materials, and Waste" category of Green Globes, Credit 5.1 Building Assemblies

provides two paths for assessing building assemblies: *5.1.1 Path A: Life Cycle Impacts for Building Assemblies* (33 out of a total 1,000 points) and *5.1.2 Path B: Materials & Product Selection for Building Assemblies* (20 out of a total 1,000 points). *5.1.1 Path A* requires either the use of Athena® Impact Estimator or a third-party peer-reviewed LCA tool that conforms to ISO 14040 and ISO 14044; example tools include GaBi and SimaPro; *5.1.2 Path B* requires Environmental Product Declarations (EPDs) that utilize recognized Product Category Rules conforming to ISO standards 14040, 14044, 14025, 21930, and EN 15840 (Type III: EPDs).

2 U.S. Green Building Council's Leadership in Energy and Environmental Design (LEED) version 4.0 introduced a new credit "Whole Building Life Cycle Assessment" in the Materials and Resources category, worth 3 points out of total 110. The goal of this credit is to conduct an LCA of the project's structure and enclosure and demonstrate a 10 percent reduction, compared with a baseline building in at least three of the six impact categories, GWP, depletion of the stratospheric ozone layer, acidification of land and water sources, eutrophication, formation of tropospheric ozone, and depletion of non-renewable energy resources.

3 Take for example the latest version of Green Globes for New Construction that offers four paths for evaluating energy performance. The four paths for Energy Performance credit in Green Globes NC are as follows: Path A: ENERGY STAR Target Finder; Path B: ASHRAE Std. 90.1–2010 Appendix G; Path C: Building Carbon Dioxide Equivalent (CO_2e) Emissions (ANSI/GBI 01–2010); and Path D: ASHRAE Building Energy Quotient (bEQ). By using one of these paths, the project can achieve points toward the Energy Performance assessment area and final Green Globes score if the associated thresholds are met. Additional information is available at: www.thegbi.org/assets/pdfs/White-Paper-Green-Globes-NC-Energy.pdf.

4 Definition of LCA from ISO 14040.

5 EIO-LCA uses producer price model with boundaries of "cradle to gate." Price models are anthropocentric since they represent the cost for resource extraction to final assembly as it leads to the factory gate. EIO-LCA is available free at www.eiolca.net.

6 Athena® Impact Estimator is a whole building, environmental LC-based decision support tool that provides a cradle-to-grave LC Inventory (LCI) profile for a whole building over a user-selected service life. A variant of this tool is the Athena® Eco-Calculator developed for the Green Building Institute for integration with its Green Globes rating system. This tool supports structural assemblies such as foundation, walls, floors, roofs, and columns and beams, and covers a total of 1,200 assemblies. Floor and ceiling finishes, site preparation and other interior furnishings are not part of the evaluation.

7 Manufacturing locations were obtained from LEED submittals for the building. DALY values/kg of emission values were obtained from Eco-Indicator 99, and Ukidwe, U. and Bakshi, B., "Thermodynamic accounting of ecosystem contribution to economic sectors with application to 1992 US economy," *Environmental Science & Technology*, 38, 2004; pp. 4810–4827.

8 A relatively new concept known as Net Zero proposes that the built environment and, by extension, building users and owners, be powered by resources from the local

environment, and preferably from the building site. In the same spirit as NZ Energy and Water, the net zero strategy can be extended to materials, emissions, and carbon as elaborated in Kibert, C.J. and Srinivasan, R.S., "Net zero: Rational performance targets for high performance buildings," in Xu J., Fry, J.A., Lev, B., Hajiyev, A. eds., *International Conference on Management Science and Engineering Management 2013*, *Lecture Notes in Electrical Engineering*, London: Springer-Verlag.

9   System boundaries include, "cradle-to-grave" – extraction to disposal; "cradle-to-gate" – extraction to warehouse prior to transporting it to building site; "cradle-to-cradle" – extraction to end-of-life, wherein, instead of disposal, the product is recycled; "gate-to-gate" – warehouse to building site and construction.

10   Previously, Dynamic-BIM (Dynamic-Building Information Modeling) platform; see Srinivasan, R.S., Kibert, C., Fishwick, P., Thakur, S., Lakshmanan, J., Ezzell, Z., Parmar, M., and Ahmed, I., "Dynamic-BIM (D-BIM) workbench for integrated building performance assessments," in *Proceedings of the Advances in Building Sciences Conference*, Madras, India, 2013; Srinivasan, R.S., Kibert, C.J., Fishwick, P., Ezzell, Z., Thakur, S., Ahmed, I., and Lakshmanan, J., "Preliminary researches in Dynamic-BIM (D-BIM) workbench development," in *Proceedings of Winter Simulation Conference*, Berlin, Germany, 2012.

Part 2

Applications

chapter 4

Emergy evaluation of mobile kiosk

To help introduce emergy analysis in the context of design and construction, it is useful to consider a simplified case. This chapter focuses on the emergy analysis of a small construction: a mobile outreach bike trailer for the University of Florida's Office of Sustainability. The project was a studio-based design-build project that involved emergy accounting of the materials involved. Due to the small scale nature of the relatively simple design, the kiosk affords a simplified, but yet detailed, emergy analysis and evaluation.

At the outset, it should be noted that the intensity of emergy analysis may vary depending on the building or building components being considered. Again, one way to understand emergy analysis is as a form of scale analysis that establishes the relative magnitude of impact for various material and energy flows in a project. Depending on the question asked of the analysis, the system boundary will vary. In the case of this relatively small project, the design-build context of the project afforded explicit accounts of the primary materials, lending itself to explicit and detailed analysis. A larger project at an earlier stage of design might start with perhaps a coarser scale of analysis to establish which components or systems might matter most as emergy flows. So, the specificity of analysis in the case of the kiosk is feasible due to the specific circumstances of the project. The methodology will be the same, but the specificity of this analysis differs from the other applications of emergy analysis considered in this book. This study focuses on the primary materials used in the construction. The aim is to establish a gauge of the total emergy of the construction itself.

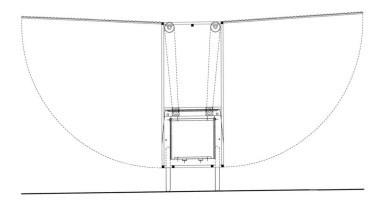

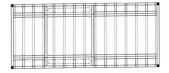

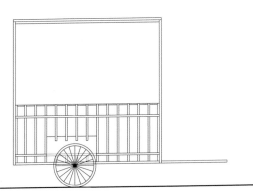

4.1 Mobile kiosk

System boundary

THE DESIGN USED REPURPOSED MATERIALS to construct a compact, portable kiosk that can expand when in use. In use, the trailer's side panels – two donated 250-watt polycarbonate photovoltaic panels – rotate up to cast shade below. The solar electricity generated is used to power LED lights, laptops, and a computer monitor that are installed in the kiosk. The primary structure for the 228-kilogram kiosk is one-inch steel tubing that was eventually finished with a powder coat. Non-ferrous metals were used for a crank system that raises and lowers the photovoltaic panels. A series of sealed Nordic birch plywood ribs support an acrylic counter for the display of information and workspace for the kiosk volunteers.

Energy systems diagram

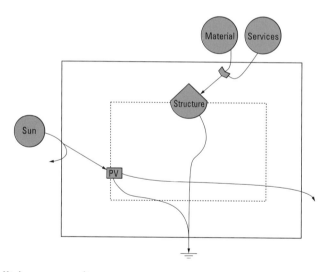

4.2 Kiosk energy systems diagram

Energy system organization

THE EMERGY ANALYSIS for this small project proceeded in two steps. First, a list of material quantities was completed (Table 4.1). Second, the total emergy quantity of the design was determined by using specific emergy (sej/g) values (Table 4.2).

Emergy evaluation table

THE EMERGY EVALUATION TABLE of mobile kiosk lists the Renewable Inputs (R) and Purchased Inputs (F) (Table 4.1). Owing to the system mobility (i.e. the kiosk is used as a mobile platform for discussing sustainable initiatives in various locations at the UF campus), for the purposes of this study, Non-renewable Inputs (N) is considered to be zero. Also, the Renewable Input to this kiosk system is the electricity generated by the PV system, over the 20-year lifetime of the PV system.

Emergy analysis

RELATIONSHIPS BETWEEN MASS and emergy are interesting to consider. The heaviest materials in the project are the non-ferrous metals used for the hand crank apparatus. This apparatus constitutes nearly half the weight of the kiosk and constitutes about a third of the total emergy (with services). The next heaviest component in the system, the steel frame, is a little over a third of the weight but reflects 45 percent of the total emergy. There is big jump to the next most significant materials in the construction. Plywood by weight is almost 9 percent of the project but only 3 percent of the emergy. Paint, a material that might otherwise be disregarded, is about 4 percent of the construction but about 14 percent of the emergy. Aluminum angles, used as a lightweight secondary structure in the roof panels, are only 1.5 percent of the project mass but represent 4 percent of the emergy in the project. All the other components constitute less than 1 percent of the mass and emergy.

Table 4.1 Kiosk emergy evaluation table

		Data		Unit Solar Emergy	Solar Emergy
		Emergy Evaluation of Mobile Sustainable University of Florida Kiosk, Gainesville, FL			
Note	Item	(units/yr)	Unit	(sej/unit)	(sej/building lifetime)
RENEWABLE INPUTS (R)					
1	Photovoltaics (on-site electricity production)	2.26E+09	j	4.16E+04	1.88E+15
	Total Renewable Inputs				1.88E+15
NON-RENEWABLE STORAGES USED (N)					
	N/A				
PURCHASED INPUTS (F)					
2	Construction Materials (except PV system)	2.32E+05	g	2.86E+10	6.63E+15
3	Construction Materials (PV systems)	3.24E+00	m²		2.07E+15
	Toal Purchased Inputs			6.40E+14	**8.71E+15**

Notes

1 Photovoltaics (on-site electricity production) (kWh generated per year)(J/kWh)(sej/J electricity output)

kWh generated per year = 6.29E+02kWh/yr (PVWATTS, 2014)

kWh/J conversion = 3.60E+06 kWh/J

Annual joules generated = 2.26E+09 J

Solar emjoules per joule of electricity = 4.16E+04 sej/J (see p.96, Note 5)

Total solar emjoules of generated electricity = 9.42E+13 sej annual energy generation

2 Construction Materials (except PV systems)

Construction energy use = (weight of building material in g)
(unit solar emergy of building material in sej/g)

3 Constuction Materials (PV systems)

Poly Si Photovaltaic modules (2 module/.5 KW)

Construction energy use of PV modules = (Total area in m²) (unit solar emergy per m² module)

Total area = 3.24E+00 m²

Unit solar emergy per m² module = 6.40E+14 sej (Raugei et al. 2007)

Total Emergy (minus labor and services) = 2.07E+15sej

Table 4.2 **Kiosk system inflows and outflow**

Renewable Inputs (R)	PV (on-site electricity production) = 1.88E+15 sej Total renewable inputs = 1.88E+5 sej
Purchased Inputs (F)	Construction materials (except PV system) = 6.63E+15 sej Construction materials (PV system) = 2.07E+15 sej Total purchased inputs = 8.71E+15 sej
Yield (Y)	Y = R + F Y = 1.88E+15 + 8.71E+15 = 1.06E+16 sej

A three-arm diagram can be used to represent the mobile kiosk (Figure 4.3). The three arms used in this diagram are the inflow (I) which is the summation of R and N; the purchased inputs (F); and total yield (Y).

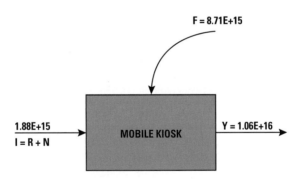

4.3 Three-arm diagram for mobile kiosk

Table 4.3 List of emergy ratios and intensive properties of mobile kiosk

Renewability (%REN)	%REN = (R + Fr)/Y %REN = (1.88E+15 + 0)/1.06E+16 = 0.18% The %REN is appreciable – the closer the %REN to 1.0, the better the system in its efficiency in processing renewable sources.
Emergy Investment Ratio (EIR)	EIR = Fn/(R + Fr + N) EIR = 8.71E+15/(1.88E+15 + 0 + 0) = 4.62 The respectable EIR of the mobile kiosk system shows the importance of renewable inputs, i.e. on-site electricity generation, in this case.
Emergy Yield Ratio (EYR)	EYR = Y/Fn EYR = 1.06E+16/8.71E+15 = 1.22
Environmental Loading Ratio	ELR = (N + Fn)/(R + Fr) ELR = (0 + 8.71E+15)/(1.88E+15 + 0) = 4.62 The value of ELR and EIR are same due to the absence of local non-renewable inputs owing to the mobility of the system.
Emergy Sustainability Index (ESI)	ESI = EYR/ELR ESI = 1.22/4.62 = 0.26 The ESI of the mobile kiosk is high due to its effective use of renewable source over its 20-year lifetime.
Emergy Density	Em Density = Y/m³ Em Density = 1.06E+20/(3.24 × 2.5) = 1.31E+15 sej/m³ Mobile kiosk area and height is 3.24 m² and 2.5 m, respectively.
Emergy Intensity	Em Intensity = Y/person Em Intensity = 1.06E+20/8 = 1.32E+15 sej/person It was assumed that up to 8 students can plug their laptops or charge their cell phones. As the PV manufacturing technology improves, more electricity can be generated for more students to take advantage, thereby reducing the emergy intensity of the kiosk.

Using these inflows and outflows, the system can be assessed using ratios and properties. Five ratios and two intensive properties are addressed in Table 4.3.

This emergy analysis considers the emergy inputs required to fabricate the project. Next steps of analysis could include the work the kiosk system is intended for, in this case the inherent emergy in the information disseminated to students on campus. Unlike in operational energy analysis, in ecological analysis the quantities *and* qualities of the system's inputs *and* outputs are of central importance. The ultimate efficacy of a system – like a building – depends on the relative power of this input, output, and feedback. So the final use, reuse, or other dissipation of the materials for this project would ultimately be included in a full evaluation of the project. For this analysis we are concerned primarily with illustrating a simplified application of the basic emergy analysis procedure. The subsequent Application example will consider more than just the basic materials of a construction assembly.

Studio faculty advisors: Charlie Hailey, Ravi Srinivasan
Studio student team: Kyle Baker, Enrique Bejarano, Travis Cmabre, Forrest Cothron, Mandy Culp, Kevin Curry, Emily Dawson, Darryl Ditzel, Arielle Elrich, Santiago Gangoyena, Roxana Hazrati, Ji Eun Hong, Richard Ledbetter, McKenzie Lentz, Critina Moreno, Channon Perry, Nicholas Ray, Genna Reckenberger, Patricia Riemer, Andres Romero, Kathleen Taus

chapter 5

Emergy evaluation of Rinker Hall

Rinker Hall is home to the University of Florida's School of Construction Management. This $6.5 million (excluding land) building was chosen by the American Institute of Architects (AIA) as one of the AIA Top Ten Environment Green Projects for 2005. It was the first U.S. Green Building Council's LEED Gold-rated building in the State of Florida under LEED-NC v.2.1. This three-story building has a floor area of about 4,390 m² (47,300 ft²). The building was built on an existing paved parking lot with a lot size of 6,879 m². Rinker Hall primarily contains classrooms, and construction and teaching laboratories on the first two floors, with offices on the third floor. Maximization of natural light in the building is achieved through the use of skylights and louvers. Motion sensors and dimmers are used to reduce electrical lighting energy consumption. Furthermore, water use is reduced by the use of low-flow plumbing fixtures, waterless urinals, and a rainwater harvesting system.

The building structure is steel-framed and the envelope consists of metal-faced composite wall panels made up of aluminum and steel sheets that enclose 1.5" thick EPS exterior insulation and finish systems (U-value = 0.062). The metal deck roof assembly has a reflective white coating on the reinforced roofing membrane. The membrane is attached to a two-inch layer of lightweight concrete and roof insulation (U-value = 0.039). The floors consist of poured concrete on steel decks and an unheated slab-on-grade at the ground floor. The exterior glazing system utilizes dual low-emissivity vertical glazing technology (U-value = 0.32, Solar Heat Gain Coefficient SHGC = 0.27, 42 percent Window Wall Ratio). This technology is additionally applied to the skylights (U-value = 0.32, SHGC = 0.27). The external doors are similarly glazed and also feature aluminum frames.

5.1 Rinker Hall at the University of Florida campus

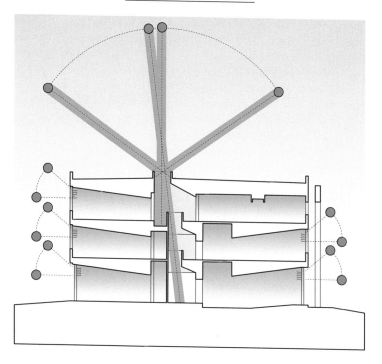

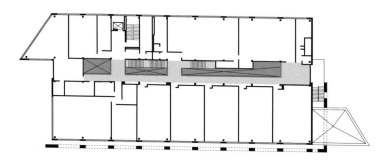

5.2 Rinker Hall section and plans

Some of Rinker Hall's bricks were recycled from another campus building that was demolished. The building design also specified the use of recycled cellulose insulation material, local and regional assembly of parts, Forest Stewardship Council certified wood, and renewable flooring material. Cooling and heating for the building is supplied by chilled water and steam, from centralized plants. These technologies and specifications are all implemented in order to minimize the environmental impact of the water, electricity, and materials used for the buildings construction and operation.

For building emergy evaluation, five distinct steps are required – the system boundary for this study: an energy system diagram representing the components and the study boundary; the energy system organization to put together an inventoried list of components and flows; the creation of an energy systems diagram; an accompanying emergy table; and the specification of indices and intensive properties used.

Step 1: System boundary

THE PURPOSE OF THIS STUDY is to analyze life cycle material, energy, potable water, and wastewater use of Rinker Hall. While major building components used in the construction, maintenance, and replacements were taken into account, the energy includes operational energy use (electricity, chilled water, steam), energy used in material transport, i.e. to jobsite or landfill post-building stage. Besides, potable water use and wastewater treatment prorated for Rinker Hall has been accounted for. The system boundary also includes the photovoltaic systems located in the site.

Step 2: Energy system diagram

ONE OF THE FIRST STEPS IN EMERGY EVALUATION is the system boundary selection and the emergy systems diagramming. Figure 5.3 shows the whole building emergy systems diagram of Rinker Hall. The sources include renewables (sun, wind, and rain) and purchased inputs (water, natural gas, electricity, materials, and services). Additionally, a photovoltaic system is installed on the site, represented as a storage, which generates electricity using the sun's renewable energy. However, the energy used from the economy in the

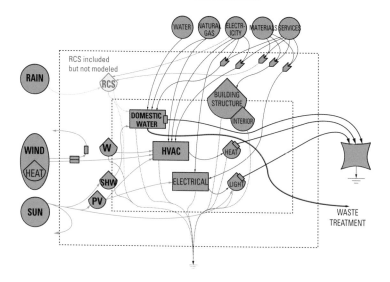

5.3 Rinker Hall emergy system diagram

manufacture of this photovoltaic system is also tracked. In other words, using emergy analysis, it is easy to track whether a renewable energy system is a source or a sink of energy just by comparing its renewable source (outputs) and purchased inputs.

Step 3: Energy system organization

IN THIS STEP, ALL RELEVANT DATA is organized by life cycle stages – Raw Material Formation and Product; Construction; Use; and Post-Building stages. For the purposes of this study, the raw material formation and product stages are combined and represented as one unit as the specific emergy values of building materials, considering both the raw material formation and product stages.

Raw material formation and product stage

For this emergy evaluation, Rinker Hall's original construction management bill of materials was used as the basis for material accounting and the emergy evaluation. The first step was to calculate the quantity (kg) of each material, which is a product of the material density (kg/m^3) and a materials volume (m^3). While material density can be located in scientific literature, material volume is calculated using the quantities thickness (m) and surface area (m^2) in the actual building assembly. The second step is to calculate the solar emergy (sej) of the material, which is the product of quantity (kg) and its corresponding unit solar emergy (sej/kg), also referred to as specific emergy of the material. Care should be taken to use unit solar emergy values derived from the same global baseline (this study uses 1.58 E25 sej/yr) due to the fact that the estimated solar transformity of a material is a function of the global baseline of analysis.

Using bills of quantities, LEED submittals, and other documents, construction material quantities are tabulated. Almost all of the construction materials may be quantified in grams (g), which then multiplied using the solar transformity (sej/g) will provide the solar emergy of the respective materials. However, there are instances where weight may be difficult to compute owing to solar transformity data availability. Take, for example, the solar emergy of solar photovoltaic systems: in the absence of detailed data to compute every individual component's emergy content, this may be determined by using existing unit solar emergy data of photovoltaic panels in sej/m^2. Also, maintenance and replacements of building components is an essential phase of a building, primarily to extend the building's lifetime whenever possible. Thus, the raw material formation and product stages track construction materials – except PV systems, construction materials of PV systems, construction materials used in maintenance and replacements.

A 4kW photovoltaic system installed outside Rinker Hall supports a small portion of the building's electricity requirement. The PV modules are composed of polycrystalline silicon. To determine the emergy content of the PV modules, Raugei et al.'s (2007)[1] specific emergy of PV modules (6.4 E+14 sej/m^2) is used. It is important to note that this value is in terms of our baseline of study, after the application of a conversion factor from the baseline used in that work. The unit of measurement used in the specific emergy of PV is the area (m^2) of the PV module. Owing to the short lifespan of PV systems, i.e. 20 years, three replacements are required, which are included in the maintenance calculation. With the increased pace in renewable technologies research, the efficiencies of PV systems are expected to improve considerably. However, for this study, the replacement energy of the PV system is maintained as a constant, i.e. a similar system is used for replacement. Although not practical, this approach is acceptable for design decision making. Additionally, renewable energy generation for 75 years is projected from the 20-year lifetime of the PV system studied and is subtracted from the electricity use over the lifetime of Rinker Hall.

Besides organizing solar emergy data by building components, it may be beneficial for some to group them into envelope and non-envelope types. This approach will help understand the emergy intensity of envelope materials that provide a thermal enclosure to the built environment. The envelope materials may then be listed in sub-categories such as groundwork, building frame, external wrapping, floors, roof, doors and windows, and sheet-metal works. Other materials such as internal walls, pavements and coverings, interior doors and windows including glazed partitions, drainage system, and interior components may be listed separately. Interior components selected for this study include HVAC metal ducts, metal blinds, tables, chairs, and white boards.

Construction stage

THE EMERGY USE RELATED TO THE TRANSPORTATION of materials from the manufacturing site to the construction site consists of material quantities, quantities of trips and mileage, and thus the amount of primary fuel used by vehicles, i.e. diesel, in this study. The distances for most of the structural components, facades, and some interior components were available from the project's LEED report.

In the case of energy used in the construction process, there was no data available. However, a few studies exist (Cole and Kernan, 1996; Scheuer et al., 2003; Athena, 1997)[2] that have previously determined that construction energy is equivalent to 4.75 percent of initial embodied energy of materials. For this study, this data was used for calculating solar emergy quantities for the construction stage. In the case of Rinker Hall, since the structure was built on an already paved area, i.e. the parking lot, soil erosion was ignored. However, if this site were on previously un-built land, soil erosion would be considered owing to permanent loss of biological systems beneath the building.

Use stage

IN THE CASE OF MAINTENANCE, if a given component's expected lifetime is less than that of the building, it is entirely replaced. For example, doors and windows typically require replacement after 40 years; so one full replacement of doors and windows is necessary during the use stage of the building. In other words, implications regarding materials with replacement times shorter than the use stage of the building will need to be included in the emergy calculation under Maintenance. For an all-inclusive study, for the replacement components, transportation energy related to product transport from manufacturing to construction site should be included. However, due to data unavailability, this study does not include transportation energies that are directly related to components replaced during the use stage. The importance of tracking all data, before construction and during the operational stage cannot be understated. For this study, we assume a 75-year use stage for this building.

To determine solar emergy of operational energy use, actual energy consumption data is required. In the case of Rinker Hall, the operational energy use data for steam (heating), chilled water (cooling), and electricity (power) were obtained from the University of Florida Physical Plant Division. A summary record depicting monthly energy consumption for 7 consecutive years for heating, cooling, and operations of the building was used to calculate annual average energy use data. This, then, was extrapolated to obtain cumulative energy use for the 75-year use stage of the building. While steam and electricity were supplied by a local utility provider, chilled water was produced on the campus using electricity. The primary fuel mix used to generate electricity and steam may be obtained from the energy provider or Economic Input-Output model – sector IDs 221300 (steam) and 221100 (electricity). For this study, the latter option was followed. The electricity generated by the PV system, beginning in 2013, was subtracted from the total electricity used by the structure during the use stage.

The emergy in water from Rinker Hall is a function of the conversion of the total gallons of water used for the year, a unit conversion of that amount into cubic centimeters which are approximately 1 gram, multiplication of this value by the transformity of water to emergy units and then an extension to the 75-year life span of the building. This can be represented, with appropriate values, in the following equation, where every constituent part is multiplied together:

$$(387{,}000) \times (3{,}785 \text{ cm}_3/\text{gal}) \times (72{,}800/\text{g}) \times (75 \text{ years})^3$$

Post-building stage

TRANSPORTATION ENERGY USED IN WASTE DISPOSAL was estimated based on local recycling and landfill facilities, as well as material quantities designated for reuse, recycling, or the landfill. Assumptions for the end-of-life stage energy included deconstruction of structural steel, facade, and some interior components, as well as the demolition of components that could not be dismantled, and transportation of deconstructed, demolished, and recyclable materials to appropriate locations.

Because one of the features of Rinker Hall's design was for its structural components and facade to be easily deconstructed, this study made the assumption that most of the structural components and facade would be reused in future construction within the campus. Also, it was assumed that the remaining miscellaneous metals, glass, concrete, gypsum board, and non-structural metal would be transported to recycling facilities within city or county limits. Therefore, the transportation energy to such facilities was estimated and included. The deconstruction and demolition energy was estimated from an Athena study done in Toronto, Canada where the energy required to deconstruct the structural steel of an office building of similar size to Rinker Hall was determined to be 130 MJ/m². The deconstruction energy was assumed to be 260 MJ/m² to account for both deconstruction and demolition energy.

Step 4: Emergy evaluation table

AN EMERGY EVALUATION TABLE is used to organize the emergy evaluation of the Rinker Hall building, see Table 5.1. The data is arranged under three major sections:

1   Renewable Inputs (R) – renewable inputs on-site from nature, namely sunlight, rain, geologic processes, and wind;
2   Non-Renewable Inputs Storages (N) – non-renewable inputs on-site such as net topsoil loss;
3   Purchased Inputs (F) – both renewable and non-renewable inputs from the economy that flows to the local site such as electricity, chilled water, steam, water, wastewater, material transport, construction materials.

In Table 5.1, the column headings comprise note, item, components (units/yr), unit, unit solar emergy (sej/unit), and solar emergy (sej/building lifetime).

Among all three sections, needless to say, the Purchased Inputs typically dominates owing to the enormous amount of material and other inputs that go into a building's structure. The solar emergy of each of the items is calculated over the lifetime of the building, i.e. 75 years, rather than on an annual basis to allow tracking of total operational energy, potable water use, and maintenance and replacements.

The Non-Renewable Storages Used relates to the local site-related inputs; in the case of a building site, this is the net topsoil loss. This relates to the inputs from the economy. For buildings, this may include energy used during operation such as electricity, chilled water, steam, water, wastewater, etc.; material transport during construction and post-building stages; and construction materials, maintenance and replacement, etc. Other than the energy purchased from the economy for building operation such as electricity, natural gas, water, etc., renewable energy systems may be used for on-site production of electricity or heat. Examples of renewable energy systems include solar photovoltaics, solar thermal systems, wind power, hydropower and marine energy, and biomass and biofuels. The actual energy used in the manufacture of such renewable energy systems should be accounted for under Purchased Inputs, particularly in the construction materials section. This is the approach taken for Rinker Hall. The only renewable energy system used in Rinker Hall is a 4 kW solar photovoltaic system.

Table 5.2 shows the total hierarchy of energy for Rinker Hall. This table shows that construction materials are the highest emergy flows in the building. Chilled water, for an air-conditioned building, represents the second most intense flow of emergy. However, a comparison of the operational emergy flows with the construction emergy flows, as in Table 5.3, reveals that the construction and maintenance of Rinker Hall dominates the hierarchy of emergy in this building. This comports with other similar comparisons. For example, Pulselli et al. found that, for buildings in Italy, for less air-conditioned buildings, the operational energy represented 15 percent of total emergy flow, while the construction and maintenance represented 84 percent of the emergy flow.[4] This observation about the hierarchy of energy in buildings – that material production, construction, and maintenance grossly outweigh operational energy – should radically shift the preoccupation of building designers from the optimization of operational energy to the larger questions about the specification of construction and the energy captured in matter.

Table 5.1 Rinker Hall emergy evaluation table and notes

Source Note	Items	Data (units/yr)	Unit	Solar Emergy (sej/building lifetime)
RENEWABLE INPUTS (R)				
1	Sunlight	4.08E+13	J	3.06E+15
2	Rain (chemical potential)	1.82E+10	J	2.47E+16
3	Wind (kinetic energy)	1.63E+11	J	1.79E+16
	Total Renewable Inputs (R)			**4.57E+16**
NON-RENEWABLE STORAGES USED (N)				
4	Net Topsoil Loss	3.11E+97	J	2.89E+14
	Total Non-Renewable Storages Used			**2.89E+14**
PURCHASED INPUTS (F)				
5	Electricity	1.64E+12	J	5.11E+18
6	Chilled Water	4.03E+12	J	1.21E+19
7	Steam	7.85E+11	J	2.88E+18
8	Water	7.24E+09	J	1.42E+16
9	Material Transport	2.48E+03	gal	1.63E+08
10	Construction Materials (except PV system)	1.80E+10	g	7.32E+19
11	Construction Materials (PV system)	1.31E+01	m²	8.38E+15
12	Construction Materials: Maintenance and Replacements (except PV system)	1.37E+09	g	4.53E+18
13	Construction Materials: Maintenance and Replacements (PV system)	2.62E+01	m²	1.68E+16
14	Construction Activities			E3.69+18
	Total Purchased Inputs			**1.02E+20**

Notes for Rinker Hall

1. Sunlight
Annual energy = (Avg. Total Annual Insolation J/yr)(Area)(1−albedo) [Odum, 1996]
Annual solar insolation = 6.90E+09 J/m²/yr [Vishner, 1954]
Site area = 6.88E+03 m²
Albedo = 0.14 [Odum, 1987]
Annual energy = 4.08E+13 J

2. Rain (chemical potential)
Annual energy = (in/yr)(Area)(0.0254 m/in)(1E6 g/m³)(4.94 J/g)(1 − runoff)
Annual rainfall = 55 in Historic 10 year average [Florida Climate Center, 2014]
Site area = 6.88E+03 m²
Runoff coefficient = 6.00E-01
Conversion factor of m/in = 2.54E-02 m/in
Conversion factor of g/m³ = 1.00E+06 g/m³
Gibbs free energy J/g = 4.74E+00 J/g
Emergy/unit = 1.81E+04 sej/J [Odum, 1996; Campbell, 2003; Campbell et al., 2004]
Annual energy = 1.82E+10 J
Annual energy = 3.30E+14 sej/J

3. Wind (kinetic energy)
Annual energy = (area)(air density)(drag coefficient)(velocity³)(sec/year) [Odum, 1996]
Site area = 6.88E+03 m²
Density of air = 1.30E+00 kg/m³
Average annual wind velocity = 5.00E+00 m/s

Table 5.1 Rinker Hall emergy evaluation table and notes – *continued*

Geostrophic wind = 8.33E+00 m/s
Drag Coefficient = 1.00E-03 [Miller, 1964 quoted by Kraus, 1972]
Sec/year = 3.14E+07
Annual energy = 1.63E+11 J
Unit solar emergy of wind = 1.47E+03 sej/J [Odum, 1996]
Annual emergy of wind = 2.39E+14 sej

4. Net Topsoil Loss
Net loss of topsoil = (farmed area)(erosion rate)
Organic matter in topsoil used up = (total mass of topsoil)(% organic)
Energy loss = (loss of organic matter)(5.4 kcal/g)(4186 J/kcal)
Erosion rate = 5 g/m²/yr [Pimentel et al., 1995]
% organic in soil = 0.04
Energy cont./g organic = 5.40 kcal/g
Annual energy = 3.11E+07 J
Unit solar emergy for net topsoil loss = 1.24E+05 sej/J [Brandt-Williams, 2002]

5. Electricity
Annual emergy = (annual energy in J)(J/kWh conversion)(unit solar emergy per Joule of the fuel
     mix used in the generation of electricity, in sej/J)
Annual energy use = 1.64E+12 J [UF PPD, 2014]
Energy mix = 77% Coal, 19% Natural gas, 4% Oil [Eco-LCA ID sector 221100]
Coal energy = 1.26E+12 J
Natural gas energy = 3.12E+11 J
Oil energy = 5.05E+10 J
Coal transformity = 4.00E+04 sej/J [Odum, 1996]
Natural gas transformity = 4.80E+04 sej/J [Odum, 1996]
Oil transformity = 5.40E+04 sej/J [Odum, 1996]
Coal emergy = 5.05E+16 sej
Natural gas emergy = 1.50E+16 sej
Oil emergy = 2.73E+15 sej
Annual electricity emergy = 6.82E+16 sej
Unit solar energy of electricity = 4.16E+04 sej/J [this study]

6. Chilled Water
Annual emergy = (annual energy in J)(unit solar emergy per Joule of the fuel mix used in
     generation of electricity used in chilled water production, in sej/J)
Annual energy use = 4.03E+12 J (Chilled water use in yr 2013) [UF PPD, 2014]
Energy mix = 77% Coal, 19% Natural gas, 4% Oil [Eco-LCA ID sector 221100]
Coal energy = 3.10E+12 J
Natural gas energy = 7.65E+11 J
Oil energy = 1.61E+11 J
Coal transformity = 4.00E+04 sej/J [Odum, 1996]
Natural gas transformity = 4.80E+04 sej/J [Odum, 1996]
Oil transformity = 5.40E+04 sej/J [Odum, 1996]
Coal emergy = 1.24E+17 sej
Natural gas emergy = 3.67E+16 sej
Oil emergy = 8.70E+15 sej
Annual chilled water emergy = 1.61E+17 sej
Unit solar emergy of chilled water = 3.99E+04 sej/J [this study]

7. Steam
Annual energy = (annual energy in J)(unit solar emergy per Joule of the fuel mix used in
     generation of electricity used in steam production, in sej/J)
Total annual energy = 7.85E+11 J
Steam energy use in yr 2013 [UF PPD, 2014]
Energy mix is19%, Coal, 41% Natural Gas, 40% Oil [Eco-LCA ID sector 221100]
Coal energy = 1.49E+11 J
Natural gas energy = 3.22E+11 J

Table 5.1 **Rinker Hall emergy evaluation table and notes** – *continued*

Oil energy = 3.14E+11 J
Coal transformity = 4.00E+04 sej/J [Odum, 1996]
Natural gas transformity = 4.80E+04 sej/J [Odum, 1996]
Oil transformity = 5.40E+04 sej/J [Odum, 1996]
Coal emergy = 5.97E+15 sej
Natural gas emergy = 1.55E+16 sej
Oil emergy = 1.70E+16 sej
Annual steam emergy = 3.84E+16 sej
Unit solar emergy of steam = 4.89E+04 sej/J [this study]

8. Water
Annual consumption = (gallons)(g/gal)(J/g)(sej/J of water) [Bastianoni et al., 2009]
Annual water consumption = 3.87E+05 gal
Water used in yr 2013 (UF PPD, 2014)
g/gal = 3.79E+03 g
J/g = 4.94E+00 J
Annual consumption in joules = 7.24E+09 J
Unit solar transformity of water = 2.61E+04 sej/J [Brown and Bardi, 2001]
Total emergy of water consumption = 1.89E+14 sej

9. Material Transport
Transportation energy use = (total diesel consumed in gal)(solar transformity of diesel in sej/J)
To job site (construction) = 1.34E+03 gal
To landfill (construction) = 1.81E+02 gal
Reused (post-building) = 2.37E+01 gal
Recycled (post-building) = 3.06E+02 gal
Landfill (post-building) = 6.28E+02 gal
Total gallons = 2.48E+03 gal
Fuel transformity = 6.58E+04 sej/J [Bastianoni et al., 2009]
Note: Material transport during maintenance and replacement not included

10. Construction Materials (except PV systems)
Construction energy use = (weight of building material in g)(unit solar emergy of building material in sej/g)

11. Construction Materials (PV systems)
Poly Si Photovaltaic modules (8 modules/4 KW)
Construction energy use of PV modules = (Total area in m^2)(unit solar emergy per m^2 module)
Total area = 1.31E+01 m^2
Unit solar emergy per m^2 module = 6.40E+14 sej [Raugei et al., 2007]
Total Emergy (minus labor and services) = 8.38E+15 sej

12. Includes pavements and coverings, doors and windows, and drainage systems

13. Construction Materials: Maintenance and Replacements (except PV systems)
PV systems lifetime = 25 yr
Number of replacements = 2

14. Construction Activities is equivalent to 4.75% of embodied energy of materials [Scheuer et al., 2003]

Table 5.2 **Rinker Hall total hierarchy of energy**

Rinker Hierarchy of Energy	
Construction Materials (except PV system)	7.32E+19
Chilled Water	1.21E+19
Electricity	5.11E+18
Replacements (except PV system)	4.53E+18
Construction Activities	3.69E+18
Steam	2.88E+18
Rain	2.47E+16
Wind	1.79E+16
Replacements (PV system)	1.68E+16
Water	1.42E+16
Construction Materials (PV system)	8.38E+15
Sunlight	3.06E+15
Net Top Solid Loss	2.89E+14
Material Transport	1.63E+08
	1.02E+20

Step 5: Emergy analysis

USING INFLOWS AND OUTFLOW tabulated in the emergy evaluation table, several analyses may be performed. Broadly speaking, two types of analysis may be relevant to buildings – ratios and intensive properties, as discussed in Fundamentals, Chapter 2. Table 5.4 lists all emergy inflows and outflow. While inflows include renewable sources, local non-renewable inputs, and purchased inputs, the total yield forms the outflow. It is to be noted that this table focuses on only inflows, i.e. no outflows have been considered, e.g. the reuse or recycling of construction materials.

Table 5.3 Rinker Hall operational versus construction energy

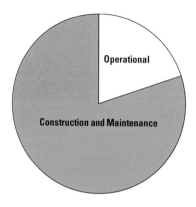

	Operational	Construction and Maintenance
Construction Materials (except PV system)		7.32E+19
Replacements (except PV system)		4.53E+18
Construction Activities		3.69E+18
Material Transport		1.63E+08
Net Topsoil Loss		2.89E+14
Construction Materials (PV system)		8.38E+15
Replacements (PV system)		1.68E+16
Chilled Water		
Electricity	1.21E+19	
Steam	5.11E+18	
Rain	2.88E+18	
Wind	2.47E+16	
Water	1.79E+16	
Sunlight	1.42E+16	
	3.06E+15	
	2.01E+19	**8.14E+19**
	19.83%	**80.17%**
	(of 1.02E+20 total building emergy)	

Table 5.4 Rinker Hall system inflows and outflow

Renewable Inputs (R)	Sunlight = 3.06E+15 sej Rain = 2.47E+16 sej Wind = 1.79E+16 sej Total renewable inputs = 4.57E+16 sej
Non-Renewable Storages Used (N)	Net topsoil loss = 2.89E+14 sej Total local non-renewable storages used = 2.89E+14 sej
Purchased Inputs (F)	No renewable inputs were used in electricity production. Chilled water and steam use electricity and natural gas respectively, both are purchased non-renewables (Fn). Moreover, the Floridan Aquifer does not replenish at the rate of use and, therefore, the source of groundwater is considered as purchased non-renewable or Fn. Diesel used in material transport and construction equipment is a purchased non-renewable similar to all other construction materials. Therefore, Fr = 0. Fr = 0 sej Fn = 8.27E+19 sej Total purchase inputs = Fr + Fn = 8.27E+19 sej
Yield (Y)	Y = R + N + F Y = 4.57E+16 + 2.89E+14 + 8.27E+19 = 8.73E+19 sej

A three-arm diagram can be used to represent the Rinker Hall building (Figure 5.4). The three arms used in this diagram are the inflow (I) which is the summation of R and N; the purchased inputs (F); and total yield (Y).

Using these inflows and outflows, the system can be assessed using ratios and properties. Five ratios are addressed in Table 5.5. This table also includes emergy space and occupant-intensive properties.

The total inflow splits in terms of percentages are: R (0.052 percent), N (0.0003 percent), and F (99.947 percent). Of the purchased inputs, construction materials possess the highest emergy. Electricity (5.04%); chilled water (11.87 percent); steam (2.84 percent); water (0.01 percent); material transport (0.001 percent); construction materials – except PV system (72.11 percent); construction materials – PV system (0.01 percent); construction materials – maintenance and replacements, except PV systems (4.46 percent); construction materials – maintenance and replacements, PV systems (0.02 percent); and

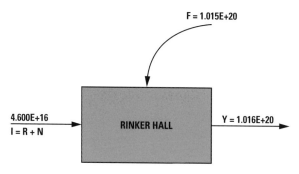

5.4 Three-arm diagram for Rinker Hall

construction activities (3.64 percent). Steel plates and poured concrete were used as flooring increasing the emergy.

Post-building stage, if a third of the construction materials are reused and another third is recycled, the emergy use scenario changes rapidly. In this scenario, no recycling and reprocessing energy is considered (see Figure 5.5 (three-arm diagram) and Table 5.6). The ⅓ reuse + ⅓ recycle scenario is evidently the best option for the following reasons: high ESI, high EYR, and high percentage REN. In terms of emergy space / occupant intensive properties, this scenario has lower Em-Density and Em-Intensity. Refer to Chapter 2 for a detailed discussion of emergy ratios.

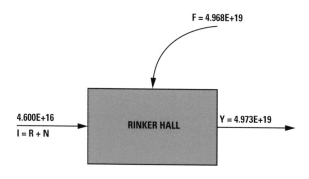

5.5 Three-arm diagram for scenario (⅓ reuse + ⅓ recycle of construction materials)

Table 5.5 List of emergy ratios and intensive properties for Rinker Hall

Renewability (%REN)	%REN = (R + Fr)/Y %REN = (4.57E+16 + 0)/1.02E+20 = 0.0005% Although the design objective suggests a high %REN, the current scenario is precarious at 0.0005%.
Emergy Investment Ratio (EIR)	EIR = Fn/(R + Fr + N) EIR = 1.02E+20/(4.57E+16 + 0 + 2.98E+14) = 2,207 The EIR is very high, essentially, investment from the purchased inputs from the economy is extremely high, i.e. the building's dependence on purchased inputs.
Emergy Yield Ratio (EYR)	EYR = Y/Fn EYR = 1.02E+20/1.02E+20 = 1.0005 With such a low EIR, the building's renewable inputs are at a very low point. In other words, the building almost entirely relies on purchased non-renewable inputs for its survival, i.e. highly inefficient.
Environmental Loading Ratio (ELR)	ELR = (N + Fn)/(R + Fr) ELR = (2.89E+14 + 1.02E+20)/(4.57E+16 + 0) = 2,221 The building's high ELR shows almost zero investment of renewable source, potentially, a debt on the environment. With increased purchased inputs with renewables and maximizing renewable source, the ELR can be reduced to a sustainable level.
Emergy Sustainability Index (ESI)	ESI = EYR/ELR ESI = 1.0005/2221 = 0.0005 The overall sustainability of the building is extremely poor, i.e. dismal performance in emergy terms. This should not be a surprise as most of the buildings designed, constructed, and operated fall in this poor performance category although they may have scored higher ratings in building rating systems. There are only two options to improve a building's ESI, namely: (i) maximize site renewable source, i.e. optimally use the site renewable source to reduce operational energy use, and (ii) consciously opt for purchased inputs with renewable inputs.
Emergy Density	Em Density = Y/m^3 Em Density = 1.02E+20/(4,390 x 4.0) = 5.78E+15 sej/m^3 Floor area and average floor-to-floor height of Rinker Hall is 4,390 m^2 and 4 m respectively.
Emergy Intensity	Em Intensity = Y/person Em Intensity = 1.02E+20/759 = 1.34E+17 sej/person Total number of occupants based on design documents is 759.

Table 5.6 Comparison of Rinker Hall indices and intensive properties with reuse + recycle scenario

Ratios	Original	1/3 Reuse + 1/3 Recycle Scenario	Improvement
%REN	0.005%	0.09%	104%
EIR	2,207	1,080	51%
EYR	1.0005	1.0009	0.05%
ELR	2,221	1,086	51%
ESI	0.0005	0.0009	104%
Em Density Y/m³	5.78E+15	2.83E+15	51%
Em Intensity Y/person	1.34E+17	6.55E+16	51%

This is exactly what has been echoed by Odum and Odum in their book, *Prosperous Way Down*, in which he focused his attention on the importance of reuse and recycling for high emergy materials.[5] In essence, through the application example of emergy analysis, architects and designers are urged:

1 To reduce the purchased input overall and to make a conscious decision in purchased inputs particularly, significantly reducing purchased inputs with non-renewables.

2 To maximize on-site renewable sources to reduce purchased inputs with non-renewables. For example, using solar thermal systems to reduce the need for natural gas for heating water, thereby increasing the use of on-site renewable source and reducing the purchased input – natural gas in this case. This is just one example, however; designers should consider the energy used up in the manufacture of renewable energy systems which will be tabulated under construction materials.

Modeling challenges and limitations

ONE OF THE MAJOR CHALLENGES that confront building stakeholders in evaluating the built environment is data collection and the scientific integrity of the methodology. The modified building cycle stage framework used in this study is an attempt to alleviate the issue of consistent system boundaries. However, modifications may be necessary depending on the system under investigation. For this particular research, the input data for emergy analysis was based on documents provided by the contractor and other reports. Although deemed sufficient for a typical emergy evaluation, they are inadequate for a comprehensive evaluation, particularly tracking of maintenance in the use stage. Moreover, there is a serious lack of research in the post-building stage, particularly into how to develop assessments for decommissioning, disposal, and reuse / recovery / recycle phases of buildings. A major limitation of emergy is its inability to calculate emissions.

Comparison of Rinker Hall emergy analysis with EIO-LCA, ATHENA® Impact Estimator, BIRDS, and Eco-LCA

FOR THIS COMPARISON, all relevant data is organized by life cycle stages – Raw Material Formation and Product; Construction; Use; and Post-Building stages. To recall, the raw material formation and product stages are combined and represented as one unit as the specific emergy values of building materials, considering both the raw material formation and product stages:

■ **Raw Material Formation and Product stage**: The raw material formation and product stages tracks sunlight, rain, wind, net topsoil loss, construction materials (except PV systems,) construction materials (PV systems), construction materials used in maintenance and replacements (except PV systems), and construction materials used in maintenance and replacements (PV systems).

■ **Construction stage**: the construction stage tracks the emergy use related to the transportation of materials from the manufacturing to the construction site, the construction site to landfill, and the energy used in the construction process itself.

■ **Use stage**: The use stage tracks operational electricity, chilled water, steam, water, and construction materials used for maintenance and replacements. For an all-inclusive study, for the replacement components, transportation energy related to product transport from manufacturing to construction site should be included. However, due to data unavailability, this study does not include transportation energies that are directly related to components replaced during the use stage.

■ **Post-building stage**: The post-building stage tracks the energy used for material transport to reuse, recycle, and landfill.

With the above structure, the energies used up during the different stages are calculated in Emergy, ATHENA® Impact Estimator, EIO-LCA, BIRDS, and Eco-LCA (Table 5.7). Refer to Chapter 3 for detailed discussion on the tools, their characteristics, and input resources.

Table 5.7 Comparison of Rinker Hall emergy analysis with EIO-LCA, ATHENA® Impact Estimator, BIRDS, and Eco-LCA

| Stage | Energy Use, TJ | | | | Used-up Energy, sej | |
	ATHENA® Impact Estimator	EIO-LCA	BIRDS	Eco-LCA	Eco-LCA	Emergy
Raw Material Formation and Product Stage	14.02	57.47		13056	2.82E+19	7.32E+19
Construction Stage	0.78	2.92		652.5	1.41E+18	3.69E+18
Use Stage	1376.38	658.76	15.34	9470	5.28E+19	2.01E+19
Post-Building Stage	0.43	0.6		17.2	6.38E+16	6.30E+07
Total	**1.39E+03**	**7.20E+02**	**1.53E+01**	**2.32E+04**	**8.25E+19**	**9.70E+19**

The application of the EIO-LCA, BIRDS, ATHENA® Impact Estimator (life cycle energy use in TJ in the models), Eco-LCA (life cycle energy use in TJ, and ECEC in sej), and emergy (life cycle emergy in sej) each present different energy-based perspectives of Rinker Hall's life cycle. In terms of energy used in TJ units, results from ATHENA® IE, EIO-LCA, BIRDS, and Eco-LCA tools are discussed below:

■ **Raw Material Formation and Product stage**: In terms of energy use (TJ), Eco-LCA shows the highest energy use. In the case of Eco-LCA, the ECEC is determined by estimating the exergy consumed by the ecological processes required to produce the raw materials, dissipate the emissions, and sustain the operation of the industrial processes. In contrast the other tools focus only on the energy used for production of the material used in the building.

- **Construction Stage**: The energy used for construction was assumed to have come primarily from diesel fuel used by construction equipment, i.e. 4.75 percent of the initial embodied energy of materials was used for the construction of structural and interior components. Transportation energy expenditure within this stage was better assessed by the ATHENA® Impact Estimator using specific project location data. However, EIO-LCA and Eco-LCA models may not be accurately modeled unless specific material transport (to construction site) data is available.

- **Use stage**: Within the Use stage, Maintenance phase, it was assumed that, if a given component's (e.g. curtain wall glazing, doors, etc.) expected useful lifespan was less than that of the building, it was entirely replaced. One of the major contributors to energy expenditures for the Maintenance phase are electrical systems, mechanical equipment, and finishes, where these products are not captured by the ATHENA® Impact Estimator. Differences in this stage using EIO-LCA and ATHENA® Impact Estimator can be attributed to the limited materials and building components included in the ATHENA® life cycle database. In the latter model, the building material database is restricted to the structural and envelope systems that are most commonly used. On the contrary, since EIO-LCA is a sector-based approach, it is not limited to the components of the building that can be included in the analysis, as long as a particular material is covered under a specific industrial sector. Therefore, EIO-LCA can provide a more thorough assessment of energy in TJ, since components such as mechanical, electrical, and plumbing can be input in the analysis, yet suffer uncertainties related to typical sector-based LCA methods.

- **Post-Building stage**: Assumptions for energy for this stage included deconstruction of structural steel, facade, and some interior components, the demolition of components that could not be dismantled, and transportation of deconstructed, demolished, and recyclable materials to appropriate locations. Because one of the features of Rinker Hall's design was for its structural components and facade to be easily deconstructed, this study made the assumption that most of the structural components and facade would be reused in future construction within the campus. Also, it was assumed that the remaining miscellaneous metals, glass, concrete, gypsum board, and non-structural metal would be transported to recycling facilities within city or county limits. Therefore, the transportation energy to such facilities was estimated and included.

In terms of emergy values, only Eco-LCA and emergy can be compared. Eco-LCA uses the U.S. Input-Output data and emergy. Among other outputs, Eco-LCA provides ECEC in sej units which can then be compared with emergy outputs. Whereas the Eco-LCA model used monetary values as inputs, emergy analysis uses material quantities and transformities. Although both methods capture the higher energy quality of, for instance, non-renewable sources of energy, i.e. solar energy required to make resources such as coal, natural gas, etc., used for electricity and heat generation (in the case of operational energy use), it is evident that there are differences between Eco-LCA and emergy results. Further investigation revealed the following reasons for the large differences in sej values between Eco-LCA and emergy:

1   The transformity values used in the emergy analysis could differ from those in Eco-LCA for the same material;
2   Emergy uses a co-product allocation rule for products of multi-output processes (e.g. co-generation of electricity and steam) whereby all the incoming energy is assigned to each product,[6] whereas Eco-LCA uses the conventional economic allocation, splitting the incoming energy based on the relative price; and
3   Eco-LCA uses the transformities developed in Zhang et al.[7] which are based on mixed baselines. Zhang et al. used transformity based on mixed emergy baselines. Besides, it was found that the assumptions about the mineral elements are that they are all the same transformity. For the comparison study between Eco-LCA and emergy to be valid, the calculations done by Eco-LCA, i.e. the database that consists of the transformities used for calculating the ECEC values, need to be redone to ensure that it uses transformities on the same baseline.

Overall, emergy analysis provides a higher quality of results owing to the intricacies of material data that can be used along with their transformities unlike the other life cycle tools that use either process or sector data. Although the process-based tools may have a slightly higher advantage in estimating life cycle energy, they, similar to their sector-based counterpart, do not track energy used in raw material formation. To overcome this issue, a new decision support tool is under development at the University of Florida that seamlessly integrates emergy and Eco-LCA. This tool will enable assessment of design decisions not only in terms of emergy values and ratios, but also will build typical LCA-based midpoint indicators and include other environmental impacts such as DALY and more.

Notes

1   Raugei, M., Bargigli, S., and Ulgiati, S., "Life cycle assessment and energy pay-back time of advanced photovoltaic modules: CdTe and CIS compared to poly-Si," *Energy*; 32, 2007; pp. 1310–1318.

2   Cole, R.J. and Kernan, P.C., "Life-cycle energy use in office buildings," *Build Environ*, 31(4), 1996; pp. 307–317; Scheuer, C., Keoleian, A., and Reppe, P., "Life cycle energy and environmental performance of a new university building: Modeling challenges and design implications," *Energy Build*, 35, 2003; pp. 1049–1064; "Demolition energy analysis of office building structural systems," Athena™ sustainable material institute, Ottawa, Canada: M. Gordon Engineering, 1997; p. 97.

3   Athena™, Sustainable material institute, "Demolition energy analysis of office building structural systems," Ottawa, Canada: M. Gordon Engineering, 1997; p.97.

4   Pulselli, R.M., Simoncini, E., and Marchinetti, N., "Energy and emergy based cost–benefit evaluation of building envelopes relative to geographical location and climate," *Building and Environment*, 44, 2009; p. 922.

5   Odum, H.T., and Odum, E.C., *A Prosperous Way Down*, Boulder, CO: University Press of Colorado, 2008.

6   Lazzaretto, A.A, "Critical comparison between thermoeconomic and emergy analyses algebra, *Energy* 34(12), 2009; pp. 2196–2205.

7   Zhang Y., Singh S., and Bakshi, B.R. "Accounting for ecosystem services in life cycle assessment, Part I: A critical review," *Environmental Science and Technology*, 44, 2010; 2232–2242. Zhang Y., Baral, A., and Bakshi, B.R., "Accounting for ecosystem services in life cycle assessment, Part II: A critical review," *Environmental Science and Technology*, 44, 2010; pp. 2624–2631.

Comprehensive list
of solar transformities

Table A.1 Comprehensive list of solar transformities

Comprehensive list: adapted from Odum (1996), Buranakarn (1998) and Others				
Item		Solar Transformity		Reference Sources
		sej/g	sej/J	
Environment				
Aggregate		1.00E+09		Odum et al., 1995 pp. 4–4, 4–5
Bauxite		8.55E+08		Odum, 1996, p. 187
Biomass – wood			3.49E+04	Odum, 1996, p. 194
Cement rock		1.00E+09		Odum, 1996, p. 310
Clay		92.00E+0		Odum, 1996, p. 310
Copper		6.80E+10		Odum et al., 1987a, p.159 Table A-1
Coral		1.00E+09		Buranakarn, 1998, Table B-1
Gypsum		1.00E+09		Brown and McClanahan, 1992, Table 2, p. 22
Iron ore		8.60E+08		Odum, 1996, p. 186
Lignite		3.70E+04		Odum, 1996, p. 186
Limestone		1.00E+09	1.62E+06	Odum, 1996, p. 46
Logs	Rainforest		3.20E+04	Odum, 1996, p. 308
	Softwood	8.01E+03		Odum, 1996, p. 80
	Hardwood	8.01E+03		Odum, 1996, p. 80
Magnesium oxide		3.80E+08		Using Chemical (Brown et al., 1992, Table A-1)
Peat			1.90E+04	Odum, 1996, p. 308
Phosphate		1.40E+10		Odum, 1996, p. 194
Plantation pine			7.00E+03	Odum, 1996, p. 308
Sand	Sand	1.00E+09	2.00E+07	Odum, 1996, p. 310
	Sandstone	1.00E+09	2.00E+07	Odum, 1996, p. 310
	Oil contaminated	1.00E+09		Buranakarn, 1998, Table B-3
Shale		1.00E+09	1.00E+07	Odum et al., 1996, p. 310
Soda ash		3.80E+08		Using Chemical (Brown et al., 1992, Table A-1)
Soil – topsoil			6.30E+04	Odum, 1996, p. 194
Uranium			1.79E+03	Odum, 1996, p. 194
Water			4.80E+04	Odum, 1996, p. 120
Zinc		6.80E+10		Odum et al., 1987a, p.159 Table A-1

Comprehensive list: adapted from Odum (1996), Buranakarn (1998) and Others				
Item		Solar Transformity		Reference Sources
		sej/g	sej/J	
Fuel and Energy				
Coal/coke			4.00E+04	Odum, 1996, p. 310
Coal/charcoal			1.06E+05	Odum, 1996, p. 308
Electricity			1.74E+05	Odum, 1996, p. 305
Liquid Fuel (waste)			6.60E+04	Using Fuel (see natural gas, petroleum gas)
LP Gas			7.00E+04	Odum et al., 1986, Table 14.1, pp. 276–282
Natural gas, petroleum gas			4.80E+04	Odum, 1996, p. 308
Oil	Crude oil	2.01E+09	5.30E+04	Odum, 1996, p. 186
	Gasoline, fuels		6.60E+04	Odum, 1996, p. 308
Oxygen		1.00E+09		Odum, 1996, p. 310
Steam			5.02E+04	Buranakarn, 1998, Table A-1
Transportation				
Trucks		9.65E11 sej/ton-mile		Buranakarn, 1998, Table E-1
		6.61E11 sej/tonne-km		Buranakarn, 1998, Table E-1
		7.55E+101.20E+06		McGrane, 1994, p. 24
Railroad (Class I)		5.07E10 sej/ton-mile		Buranakarn, 1998, Table E-2
		3.47E10 sej/tonne-km		Buranakarn, 1998, Table E-2
		4.55E+098.70E+06		McGrane, 1994, p. 40
		3.70E10 sej/ton-mile		Updated in Buranakarn, 1998 (adapted from Bayley et al., 1977)
Ships (US domestic)		1.17E11 sej/ton-mile		Buranakarn, 1998, Table E-3
		7.99E10 sej/tonne-km		Buranakarn, 1998, Table E-3
		7.55E10 sej/ton-mile		Updated in Buranakarn, 1998 (adapted from Bayley et al., 1977)

Comprehensive list: adapted from Odum (1996), Buranakarn (1998) and Others				
Item		Solar Transformity		Reference Sources
		sej/g	sej/J	
Machinery, Equipment & Process				
Machinery		6.70E+09		Odum et al., 1987b, Table 1, pp. 4–5
Demolition (concrete)		4.87E+07		Buranakarn, 1998, Table D-6
Crushing (concrete)		1.66E+07		Buranakarn, 1998, Table D-8
Collection (post-consumer product)		2.51E+08		Buranakarn, 1998, Table D-1
Separation (post-consumer product)		8.24E+06		Buranakarn, 1998, Table D-3
Products				
Aluminum	Ingots	1.63E+10		Odum et al., 1995b, p. B2; Odum et al., 1983, Table 3.1, pp. 40–45
	Primary – ingots (w/ services)	1.17E+10	1.79E+08	Buranakarn, 1998, Table C-7
	Primary – ingots (w/o services)	1.14E+10	1.75E+08	Buranakarn, 1998, Table C-7
	Sheet (w/ services)	1.27E+10		Buranakarn, 1998, Table 3.6
	Sheet (w/o services)	1.27E+10		Buranakarn, 1998, Table 3.6
	Sheet – material recycle (w/ services)	1.30E+10		Buranakarn, 1998, Table 3.6
	Sheet – material recycle (w/o services)	1.30E+10		Buranakarn, 1998, Table 3.6
	Sheet – material recycle and byproduct (w/ services)	1.29E+10	1.98E+08	Buranakarn, 1998, Table 3.6
	Sheet – material recycle and byproduct (w/o services)	1.29E+10	1.97E+08	Buranakarn, 1998, Table 3.6

Comprehensive list: adapted from Odum (1996), Buranakarn (1998) and Others				
Item		Solar Transformity		Reference Sources
		sej/g	sej/J	
Ammonia fertilizer		3.80E+09	1.86E+06	Odum, 1996, p. 310
Brick	(w/ services)	2.20E+09		Buranakarn, 1998, Table 3.3
	(w/o services)	2.19E+09		Buranakarn, 1998, Table 3.3
	With sawdust fuel (w/ services)	2.12E+09		Buranakarn, 1998, Table 3.3
	With sawdust fuel (w/o services)	2.04E+09		Buranakarn, 1998, Table 3.3
	With oil contaminated soil and sawdust fuel (w/ services)	1.93E+09		Buranakarn, 1998, Table 3.3
	With oil contaminated soil and sawdust fuel (w/o services)	1.90E+09		Buranakarn, 1998, Table 3.3
	And structural clay tile (w/ services)	2.32E+09		Buranakarn, 1998, Table C-13
	And structural clay tile (w/o services)	2.23E+09		Buranakarn, 1998, Table C-13
Cement		2.31E+09		Updated in Buranakarn, 1998, (adapted from Haukoos, 1995, Table A13, p. 172, w/o service)
	Without fly ash (w/ services)	1.98E+09		Buranakarn, 1998, Table 3.1
	Without fly ash (w/o services)	1.97E+09		Buranakarn, 1998, Table 3.1
	With fly ash (w/ services)	2.20E+09		Buranakarn, 1998, Table 3.1
	With fly ash (w/o services)	2.19E+09		Buranakarn, 1998, Table 3.1
Chemical		3.80E+08		Odum et al., 1987a, p.159 Table A-1
Chemical products			3.45E+04	Odum et al., 1983, Table 11.1, pp. 207–215

Comprehensive list: adapted from Odum (1996), Buranakarn (1998) and Others				
Item		Solar Transformity		Reference Sources
		sej/g	sej/J	
Concrete	Readymix (w/ services)	1.44E+09		Buranakarn, 1998, Table 3.2
	Readymix (w/o services)	1.44E+09		Buranakarn, 1998, Table 3.2
	Readymix with fly ash (w/ services)	1.55E+09		Buranakarn, 1998, Table 3.2
	Readymix with fly ash (w/o services)	1.54E+09		Buranakarn, 1998, Table 3.2
	Readymix with recycled concrete aggregate (w/ services)	1.59E+09		Buranakarn, 1998, Table 3.2
	Readymix with recycled concrete aggregate (w/o services)	1.59E+09		Buranakarn, 1998, Table 3.2
	Crushed (w/ services)	4.28E+09		Buranakarn, 1998, Table D-8
	Crushed (w/o services)	4.82E+09		Buranakarn, 1998, Table D-8
	Block	1.35E+09		Haukoos, 1995, Table A-15, pp. 177–179 w/ services
Copper and zinc alloys (MSW)		6.77E+10		Odum et al., 1987a, p. 159
Explosives (as ammonium nitrate fertilizer)		3.80E+09	1.86E+06	Using Ammonia Fertilizer (Odum, 1996, p. 310)
Ferrous metals (MSW)		9.18E+08		Odum et al., 1987a, p. 159

Comprehensive list: adapted from Odum (1996), Buranakarn (1998) and Others				
Item		Solar Transformity		Reference Sources
		sej/g	sej/J	
Fiberboard production (1972)		1.84+09	1.12E+05	Updated in Buranakarn, 1998 (adapted from Haukoos, 1995, Table A7, pp. 157–158, w/o services)
		2.40E+09	1.58E+05	Updated in Buranakarn, 1998 (adapted from Haukoos, 1995, Table A7, pp. 157–158, w/ services)
Flooring	And sliding (w/ services)	8.79E+08	4.20E+04	Buranakarn, 1998, Table 3-9
	And sliding (w/o services)	8.33E+08	3.98E+04	Buranakarn, 1998, Table 3-9
	Vinyl – PVC (w/ services)	6.32E+09	1.94E+05	Buranakarn, 1998, Table 3-11
	Vinyl – PVC (w/o services)	6.02E+09	1.85E+05	Buranakarn, 1998, Table 3-11
Flyash		1.40E+10		Buranakarn, 1998, Table C-1
Food			2.00E+06	Odum et al., 1987a, p.159 Table C-7
Food waste (MSW)			1.80E+06	Odum et al., 1987a, p. 159

Comprehensive list: adapted from Odum (1996), Buranakarn (1998) and Others				
Item		Solar Transformity		Reference Sources
		sej/g	sej/J	
Glass	(MSW)	8.44E+08		Odum et al., 1987a, p.159
	Flat	4.74E+09		Updated in Buranakarn, 1998 (adapted from Haukoos, 1995, Table A16, pp. 180–182, w/ services)
	Flat – 1987 (w/ services)	1.90E+09	1.37E+07	Buranakarn, 1998, Table C-12
	Flat – 1987 (w/o services)	1.60E+09	1.15E+07	Buranakarn, 1998, Table C-12
	Post consumer (w/ services)	2.13E+09	1.53E+07	Buranakarn, 1998, Table D-4
	Post consumer (w/o services)	2.12E+09	1.52E+07	Buranakarn, 1998, Table D-4
	Windshield (post-consumer)	1.90E+09		Buranakarn, 1998, Table C-12
	Float (w/ services)	7.87E+09		Buranakarn, 1998, Table 3-14
	Float (w/o services)	7.68E+09		Buranakarn, 1998, Table 3-14
	Float with recycled inhouse new glass scrap (w/ services)	7.66E+09	5.51E+07	Buranakarn, 1998, Table 3-14
	Float with recycled inhouse new glass scrap (w/o services)	7.47E+09	5.37E+07	Buranakarn, 1998, Table 3-14
Glue and adhesives		3.80E+08		Using Chemical (Brown et al., 1992, Table A-1)
Hardboard production (split products)		1.92E+09	1.27E+05	Updated in Buranakarn, 1998 (adapted from Haukoos, 1995, Table A9, pp. 161–162, w/o services)
HDPE (w/o services)		5.27E+09	1.62E+05	Buranakarn, 1998, Table C-10

Comprehensive list: adapted from Odum (1996), Buranakarn (1998) and Others				
Item		Solar Transformity		Reference Sources
		sej/g	sej/J	
Iron	Pig iron (w/ services)	2.83E+09	4.06E+06	Buranakarn, 1998, Table C-3
	Pig iron (w/o services)	2.65E+09	3.80E+06	Buranakarn, 1998, Table C-3
Lumber	Softwood	1.77E+09	4.40E+04	Updated in Buranakarn, 1998, (adapted from Haukoos, 1995, Table A-2a, pp. 139–140); Odum, 1996, p. 308
	(w/ services)	8.79E+08	4.20E+04	Buranakarn, 1998, Table C-9
	(w/o services)	8.33E+08	3.98E+04	Buranakarn, 1998, Table C-9
	With plastic – HDPE (w/ services)	5.75E+09		Buranakarn, 1998, Table 3-12
	With plastic – HDPE (w/o services)	5.04E+09		Buranakarn, 1998, Table 3-12
	With plastic – HDPE – adaptive reuse (w/ services)	6.33E+09	1.95E+05	Buranakarn, 1998, Table 3-12
	With plastic – HDPE – adaptive reuse (w/o services)	5.61E+09	1.73E+05	Buranakarn, 1998, Table 3-12
	With wood and recycled (w/ services)	6.74E+09		Buranakarn, 1998, Table 3-10
	With wood and recycled (w/o services)	1.77E+09		Buranakarn, 1998, Table 3-10
	With shaved (using wood chips)	8.79E+08		Buranakarn, 1998, Table 3-9
	With shaved	1.63E+09		Updated in Buranakarn, 1998, (adapted from Haukoos, 1995, Table A-4a, pp. 147–148)
Paper			1.42E+05	Keller, 1992, p 116
Particleboard production (1972)		1.57E+09	1.04E+05	Updated in Buranakarn, 1998, (adapted from Haukoos, 1995, Table A6, pp. 155–156, w/o services)

Comprehensive list: adapted from Odum (1996), Buranakarn (1998) and Others			
Item		Solar Transformity	Reference Sources
		sej/g	sej/J	
Rubber			2.10E+04	Odum et al., 1983, Table 3.1, pp. 40–45
	(MSW)	4.30E+09		Odum et al., 1987a, p.159
Slag	(w/ services)	7.06E+09	1.10E+07	Buranakarn, 1998, Table C-3
	(w/o services)	6.61E+09	9.50E+06	Buranakarn, 1998, Table C-3
Sodium		1.10E+09		Using Potassium
Steel		1.78E+09		Odum, 1996, p. 186
	EAF process (w/ services)	4.15E+09		Buranakarn, 1998, Table 3.4
	EAF process (w/o services)	4.10E+09		Buranakarn, 1998, Table 3.4
	EAF process – material recycle (w/ services)	4.41E+09		Buranakarn, 1998, Table 3.4
	EAF process – material recycle (w/o services)	4.37E+09		Buranakarn, 1998, Table 3.4
	EAF process – material recycle and byproduct (w/ services)	4.24E+09	6.09E+06	Buranakarn, 1998, Table 3.4
	EAF process – material recycle and byproduct (w/o services)	4.19E+09	6.03E+06	Buranakarn, 1998, Table 3.4
	BOF process (w/ services)	5.35E+09		Buranakarn, 1998, Table 3.4
	BOF process (w/o services)	5.31E+09		Buranakarn, 1998, Table 3.4
	BOF process – material recycle (w/ services)	5.35E+09	7.69E+06	Buranakarn, 1998, Table 3.5
	BOF process – material recycle (w/o services)	5.31E+09	7.62E+06	Buranakarn, 1998, Table 3.5

Comprehensive list: adapted from Odum (1996), Buranakarn (1998) and Others			
Item		Solar Transformity		Reference Sources
		sej/g	sej/J	
Textiles (MSW)			3.80E+06	Odum et al., 1987a, p. 159
Tile	Ceramic (w/ services)	3.06E+09		Buranakarn, 1998, Table 3-13
	Ceramic (w/o services)	2.86E+09		Buranakarn, 1998, Table 3-13
	Ceramic with windshield glass (w/ services)	3.42E+09		Buranakarn, 1998, Table 3-13
	Ceramic with windshield glass (w/o services)	3.22E+09		Buranakarn, 1998, Table 3-13
	Ceramic with post consumer glass bottles (w/ services)	3.38E+09		Buranakarn, 1998, Table 3-13
	Ceramic with post consumer glass bottles (w/o services)	3.19E+09		Buranakarn, 1998, Table 3-13
Tire (waste)			2.10E+04	Using Rubber (Odum et al., 1983, Table 3.1, pp. 40–45)
Veneer	Softwood		4.40E+04	Odum, 1996, p. 308
	Softwood (w/ services)	1.21E+09	5.77E+04	Buranakarn, 1998, Table 3-7
	Softwood (w/o services)	1.12E+09	5.33E+04	Buranakarn, 1998, Table 3-7
	Hardwood		4.40E+04	Odum, 1996, p. 308
	Hardwood (w/ services)	1.44E+09	6.90E+04	Buranakarn, 1998, Table C-16
	Hardwood (w/ services)	1.25E+09	6.00E+04	
Wood	Chips		1.56E+04	Doherty, 1995, p. 145
	Chips (w/ services)	8.79E+08	4.20E+04	Buranakarn, 1998, Table 3-9
	Chips (w/o services)	8.33E+08	3.98E+04	Buranakarn, 1998, Table 3-9
	Harvested		8.01E+03	Odum, 1996, p. 80
	Rainforest (transported and chipped)		4.40E+04	Odum, 1996, p. 308
	Fiber (15–18% content)		4.20E+04	Buranakarn, 1998, Table 3-9

Comprehensive list: adapted from Odum (1996), Buranakarn (1998) and Others			
Item		Solar Transformity		Reference Sources
		sej/g	sej/J	
Yard-wood trimmings (MSW)			4.30E+03	Odum et al., 1987a, p. 159
Services				
Labor (primitive)			8.10E+04	Odum, 1996, p. 68
Labor (1983)	2.40E+12 sej/$			Odum, 1996, Table D-1, p. 314
Labor (1993)	1.37E+12 sej/$			Odum, 1996, Table D-1, p. 314

Table A.2 Completed emergy evaluation table for Colorado mountain building

Colorado Mountain Building	Total Mass (g)	Specific Emergy (sej/g) w/ services	Specific Emergy (sej/g) w/o services	Emergy (sej) w/ services	Emergy (sej) w/o services
Softwood	9,495,528	8.79E+08	8.33E+08	8.35E+15	7.91E+15
Plywood	356,637	1.44E+09	1.25E+09	5.14E+14	4.46E+14
Steel (BOF recycled)	2,019,411	5.35E+09	5.31E+09	1.08E+16	1.07E+16
Concrete	8,708,966	1.44E+09	1.44E+09	1.25E+16	1.25E+16
Glass (float)	410,214	7.87E+09	7.68E+09	3.23E+15	3.15E+15
Roof membrane	187,073	4.30E+09	n/a	8.04E+14	n/a

Glossary

Amplifier: an interacting agent in a system that increases the power of the system.

Available energy: energy in a system that can perform work; will be degraded (change in quality) in the process of work. Available energy and exergy are synonymous terms.

Boundary: that which separates a system and its surroundings; a zone of change and exchange; the event-space where energy and matter is exchanged across a boundary; together the system, the boundary, and the surroundings constitute an energy system.

Closed system: a system, as defined by its boundary, is open to energy exchange with its surroundings but not material exchange.

Consumers: system components in an energy system that intake more energy than they output; they transform energy quality, store it, and feed back in the system.

Dissipation: the irreversible flux and transformations of energy in a system.

Dissipative structure: a non-isolated, far from equilibrium thermodynamic system that yields quasi-steady-state conditions through exchange of matter and energy with its surroundings.

Donor value: refers to all the value of the required energetic contributions of a process, product, or service – understood in contrast to the resulting market value or receiver value of that process, product, or service.

Emergy: the available energy of one form that is used up in transformations directly and indirectly to make a product or service.

Emergy density: emergy per unit density of a material.

Emergy yield ratio: emergy consumed to emergy invested.

Empower: flow of emergy per unit time.

Empower density: emergy per unit time and unit volume.

Energy: a property that can be converted to heat; a measure of the capacity of a system to do work on its surroundings.

Energy gradient: a difference between maximal and minimal available energy states.

Energy transformation hierarchy: the hierarchical organization of energy flows; the position of any entity in a system is measured in transformities.

Environmental loading ratio: non-renewable energy to renewable energy consumed.

Exergy: the available energy in a system, a measure of the maximum work potential in a system before it reaches equilibrium.

Extensive property: a physical property of a system that is proportional to the amount of material in the system.

Externality: a system cost that affects the system but was ignored in design or analysis; that which is constitutively excluded from consideration but that is nonetheless inherent in the systems. A "net zero" building, for instance, externalizes many energetic costs to make its "net zero" claim.

Feedback reinforcement: emergy flowing back through an energy hierarchy has the capacity to reinforce the power of the system.

Gross emergy product: total emergy required to drive a national economy.

Hierarchy of energy: the hierarchy of energy systems that evolve over time through self-organization; energy converges through successive transformations to yield spatial and temporal hierarchies of energy structure into increasingly higher quality quantities that have greater capacity to interact and guide lower quality entities through system feedback.

High quality energy: high emergy forms of energy that are capable of many types of work.

Intensive property: a physical property of a system that does not depend on the system size or the amount of material in the system.

Interaction: component that combines two or more lower quality inputs for a higher quality output.

Isolated system: a system, as defined by its boundary, is open to neither energy exchange with its surroundings nor material exchange; the universe as a whole might be an isolated system.

Low quality energy: energy that has limited capacity for work on its surroundings.

Maximum empower principle: in self-organized systems, designs that maximize intake, transformation, and feedback reinforcement will prevail.

Maximum entropy production: the systems which prevail in a process of natural selection will be those designs that extract maximal power from an available energy gradient and in so doing maximize the production of entropy, thus reradiating remaining energy at the lowest possible level.

Maximum power: during self-organization processes, systems develop and prevail that maximize power intake and the transformation of that energy, and that reinforce production through feedback.

Non-isolated: thermodynamic systems are either isolated (no material or energy exchanges with its surroundings), closed (no material exchanges with its surroundings), or open (material and energy exchanges with surroundings are constitutive). Non-isolated refers to systems that exchange at least energy, if not matter as well. Bodies, buildings, and cities are all non-isolated systems.

Non-linear, Non-equilibrium thermodynamics: to be distinguished from classical, linear thermodynamics, the branch of thermodynamics focused on systems that persist far from equilibrium.

Open system: a system, as defined by its boundary, that is open to energy and material exchange with its surroundings; all bodies, buildings, and cities are open systems.

Power: the rate at which work is done; the rate at which energy is consumed; useful energy flux per unit of time.

Producer: a system component that captures and transforms diffuse, low quality energy to create higher quality products, under the control of high quality inputs. A tree is one example.

Pulsing: the changing organization of energy systems over time to achieve maximum power.

Reinforcement: feedback; a system action that serves to enhance system production through a loop of mutually enhancing co-evolution.

Second law of thermodynamics: the universal energy principle which states that concentrations spontaneously dissipate towards a state of equilibrium; the universal tendency for available energy gradients to dissipate.

Self-organization: the use of energy to develop and evolve system structure and organization.

Sink: a component in an energy system that maintains more incoming energy than outgoing energy.

Solar emergy: use of solar energy as the basis of emergy analysis; the available solar energy that is used up in transformations directly and indirectly to make a product or service.

Solar empower: solar emergy per unit of time.

Solar transformity: Solar emergy per unit of energy as expressed in solar emjoules per joule (sej/J).

Source: energy inputs into a system.

Specific emergy: emergy input / investment required for a unit of mass output.

Storage: an energy system component that stores a quantity of energy; necessarily represents a balance of inflow and outflow.

Surrounding: that which surrounds a system, as separated by a boundary; together the system, the boundary, and the surroundings constitute an energy system.

System: the organization of energy and / or matter that is the focus of study; together the system, the boundary, and the surroundings constitute an energy system.

Transformity: emergy input required per unit of available energy output.

Unavailable energy: energy in a system that can no longer do work; entropy.

Useful energy: exergy that serves to increase system functioning.

Work: a change in energy concentration or form as a result of an energy transformation.

Annotated bibliography

This appendix is a comprehensive set of references to the extant literature on emergy systems in architecture and its associated implications. To help organize these resources, we have first organized the references into distinct categories. Then, within each category, we have annotated some of the primary references to provide another level of hierarchy.

Citations for tables

Bastianoni, S., Pulselli, R.M., Pulselli, F.M., "Models of Withdrawing Renewable and Non-renewable resources based on Odum's energy systems theory and Daly's Quasi-Sustainability Principle." In: Ecological Modelling 220, 2009: 1926–1930.

Bayley, S.E., Odum, H.T., and Kemp, W.M., (1977). *Energy evaluation and management alternatives for Florida's east coast. In Transcript of the 41st North American Wildlife Conference.* Washington DC: Wildlife Management Institute, 1997.

Bayley, S., Zucchetto, J., Shapiro, L., Mall, D., and Nessel, J., "Energetics and Systems Modeling: A Framework Study for Energy Evaluation of Alternative Transportation Modes." U.S. Army Engineer Institute for Warer Resources (IWR). December 1977. Contract Number DACW 17-75-0075.

Brandt-Williams, S., "Emergy of Florida Agriculture, Folio #4, Handbook of Emergy Evaluation: A compendium of data for emergy computation issued in a series of folios," Center for Environmental Policy, Department of Environmental Engineering Sciences, University of Florida, Gainesville, Florida, 2002; p.40.

Brown M.T. and Bardi E., "Emergy of Ecosystems, Folio #3" Handbook of Emergy Evaluation," Center for Environmental Policy, Environmental Engineering Sciences, University of Florida, Gainesville, FL. July 2001.

Brown, M.T. and McClanahan, T.R, *Emergy Analysis Perspectives of Thailand and Mekong River Dam Proposals. Report to the Cousteau Society.* Center for Wetlands and Water Resources, University of Florida, Gainesville, FL, 1992.

Buranakarn, V., *Evaluation of Recycling and Reuse of Building Materials Using the Emergy Analysis Method*, Ph.D. Dissertation, University of Florida, 1998.

Campell, D.E., "A Note on the uncertainty in estimates of Transformities Based on Global Water Budget," pp. 349-353. In Brown, M.T., Odum, H.T., Tilley, D.R., Ulgiati, S. (eds) *Emergy Synthesis 2*. Proceedings of the Second Biennial Emergy Analysis Conference. Center for Environmental Policy, University of Florida, Gainesville, 2003.

Campbell, D.E, Meisch, M., Demoss, T., Pomponio, J., Bradley, M.P, Keeping the books for environmental systems: an emergy analysis of West Virginia." Journal of Environmental monitoring and assessment, Volume 94, issue 1-3, 2004; pp. 217–230.

Doherty, S. J., *Emergy evaluations of and limits to forest production*. Ph.D. Dissertation, University of Florida, 1995.

Florida Climate Center: Florida State University. The Florida Climate Center, Total Precipitation Measurements. Office of the state climatologist. 2014. Retrieved from: http://climatecenter.fsu.edu/climate-data-access-tools/climate-data-visualization

Haukoos, D.S., "Sustainable Architecture and its Relationship to Industrialized Building." MS thesis, University of Florida, Gainesville, 1995.

Keller, P. A., *Perspectives on Interfacing Paper Mill Wastewaters and Wetlands*. MS thesis, University of Florida, Gainesville, 1992.

Kraus, E.B., Atmosphere-Ocean Interaction, Clarendon Press, Oxford, 1972.

McGrane, G., An *emergy evaluation of personal transportation alternatives*. M.S. Thesis. University of Florida, Gainesville, FL, 1994.

Odum, H.T., *Systems Ecology: An Introduction*. New York: John Wiley, 1983.

Odum, Howard T., Elisabeth C. Odum, Gisela Bosch, Leon C. Braat, William Dunn, Gordon De R. Innes, John R. Richardson, David M. Scienceman, Jan P Sendzimjr, David J. Smith, and Michael V. Thomas. *Energy Analysis Overview of Nations.* September 1983. WP-83-82. International Institute for Applied Systems Analysis. A-2361 Luxemburg, Austria, 1983.

Odum, H.T., Odum, E.C., King, R.,and Richardson, R., *Ecology and Economy: "Emergy" Analysis and Public Policy in Texas.* Energy Systems in Texas and The United States, Policy Research Project Report Number 78. The Board of Regents, The University of Texas, 1987a; p 159.

Odum, Howard. T., Flora C. Wang, John F. Alexander, Jr.., Martha Gilliland, Mike Miller, and Jan Sendzimer. *Energy Analysis of Environmental Value.* Center for Wetlands, University of Florida, Publication #78-17, 1987b.

Odum, H.T., Brown, M.T. , McGrane, G., Woithe, R.D., Lopez, S., and Bastianoni, S., *Emergy Evaluation of Energy Policies for Florida. Final Report.* January 1995. Center for Environmental Policy, Department of Environmental Engineering Science, University of Florida, 1995.

Odum, H.T., (1996). *Environmental Accounting: Emergy and Decision Making.* New York: John Wiley.

Pimentel, D., Harvey, C., Resosudarmo, P., Sinclair, K., Kurz, D., McNair, M., Crist, S., Shprotz, L., Fitton, L., Saffouri, R. and Blair, R.: 1995, 'Environmental and economic costs of soil erosion and conservation benefits', Science 267, 1117–1121.

UF PPD., Personal interview with Dustin Stephany, Department of Energy, University of Florida, 2014

Emergy of buildings and building materials

Amponsah, N.Y., Lacarrière, B., Jamali-Zghal, N., and Le Corre, O., "Impact of building material recycle or reuse on selected emergy ratios," Resources, Conservation and Recycling, 67, 2012; pp. 9–17.
Consideration of recycling processes in various building material streams and their effect in various thermodynamic indicators. There is a focus on the emergetic changes associated with repeated recycling of materials. The

aim is to develop a methodology to prioritize materials for recycling and the number of times a material should be recycled.

Buranakarn, V. *Evaluation of Recycling and Reuse of Building Materials Using the Emergy Analysis Method*, Ph.D. Dissertation, University of Florida, 1998.
This dissertation provided the basis for many building emergy assessments. The focus is on six primary building materials and a number of secondary materials used in construction. It includes consideration of a variety of recycling streams for these materials as well.

Kilbert, C.J., Sendzimir, J., and Guy, G.B., eds. *Construction Ecology: Nature as the Basis of Green Buildings*. London: Spon Press, 2002.
Important book that expanded the discourse on energy and materials in architecture by applying principles of industrial ecology and ecosystem science to the construction industry. The book includes several important chapters, listed elsewhere in this bibliography.

Meillaud, F., Gay, J.B., and Brown, M.T., "Evaluation of a building using the emergy method," *Solar Energy*, 79(2), 2005; pp. 204–212.
An early full building emergy analysis of a higher education research facility in Lausanne, Switzerland. The significant role of people and information in the building is compared to the constructional and operational emergy.

Pulselli, R.M., Simoncini, E., and Marchettini, N., "Energy and emergy based cost–benefit evaluation of building envelopes relative to geographical location and climate," *Building and Environment*, 44(5), 2009; pp. 920–928.
This article presents a comparison of three envelope types (cavity wall, insulated, and ventilated). Both emergy analysis and energy analysis are used to evaluate operational and construction costs of the respective envelope systems.

Pulselli, R.M., Simoncini, E., Pulselli, F.M., and Bastianoni, S., "Emergy analysis of building manufacturing, maintenance and use: Em-building indices to evaluate housing sustainability," *Energy and Buildings*, 39(5), 2007; pp. 620–628.
The focus of this article is on the relative costs for the manufacture, maintenance, and use of building materials in a prototypical housing building. The authors use a range of building-specific indices such as emergy of building manufacture, emergy per building volume, emergy analysis of building use, and emergy per person.

Pulselli, R.M., Simoncini, E., Ridolfi, R., and Bastianoni, S., "Specific emergy of cement and concrete: An energy-based appraisal of building materials and their transport," *Ecological Indicators*, 8(5), 2008; pp. 647–656.

An in-depth consideration of a single material – concrete – in the context of Italy. Each step of the manufacture process is considered using an emergy methodology. The authors use an Emergy Investment Ratio (EIR) as a synthetic indicator of ecological efficacy.

Srinivasan, R.S., *Re(de)fining Net Zero Energy: Renewable Emergy Balance of Environmental Building Design*, Ph.D. Dissertation, University of Pennsylvania, 2011.

This dissertation develops a method to maximize renewable resource use through emergy analysis to close the gap between current approaches to environmental building design and the over-arching goal of creating buildings that contribute to the sustainability of the geobiosphere. The objective of this study is to assess the performance of built systems and identify the maximum potential bounds for renewable resource substitution within the building process.

Srinivasan, R.S., Braham, W.W., Campbell, D.E., and Curcija, C.D., "Building envelope optimization using emergy analysis," *Proceedings of Building Simulation 2011: 12th Conference of International Building Performance Simulation Association, Sydney, 14–16 November*.

Presents a workflow for integrating emergy analysis and energy optimization techniques for the evaluation of a typical building envelope system. As such, optimal insulation quantities, rather than maximal insulation quantities, are selected.

Srinivasan, R.S., Ingwersen, W., Trucco, C., Ries, R., and Campbell, D. "Incorporating impacts on ecosystem services into life cycle assessment for built environments," *Building and Environment Journal*, 2014; pp. 138–151.

Economic, social and cultural considerations

Abel, T., "Complex adaptive systems, evolutionism, and ecology within anthropology: Interdisciplinary research for understanding cultural and ecological dynamics," *Journal of Ecological Anthropology*, 2, 1998; pp. 6–29.

Abel, T., "Understanding complex human ecosystems: The case of ecotourism on Bonaire," *Ecology and Society*, 7(3), 2003; pp. 2112–2117.

Abel, T., "Systems diagrams for visualizing macroeconomics," *Ecological Modelling*, 178(1), 2004; pp. 189–194.
This short article situates macroeconomics and emergy analysis of human society through a hierarchy of the household as an economic / ecological unit. It exposes the limits of classical macroeconomic thinking regarding the topics of "labor" and "natural resources."

Abel, T., "Emergy, sociocultural hierarchy, and cultural evolution," *Emergy Synthesis 4: Theory and Applications of the Emergy Methodology. Proceedings from the Fourth Emergy Conference*, 2007; pp. 28.1–28.14.
In spatial and material terms, emergy analysis is the basis for understanding the evolution of human sociocultural hierarchies. This chapter uses the household as an emergetic unit of society.

Abel, T., "Human transformities in a global hierarchy: Emergy and scale in the production of people and culture," *Ecological Modelling*, 221(17), 2010; pp. 2112–2117.
This article reflects an evaluation and refinement of human labor transformities. The resulting values help situate the role of humans in their larger energy hierarchies.

Abel, T., "Culture in cycles: Considering H.T. Odum's 'information cycle,'" *International Journal of General Systems*, 43, 2013; pp. 1–31.
Important assessment of the role that information plays in large scale systems, especially human cultural systems. There is an emphasis on the importance of information cycling to direct the energy transformation, available gradient reduction functions, and the development of auto-catalytic dissipative structures in human systems.

Bonilla, S.H., Guarnetti, R.L., Almeida, C.M.V.B., and Giannetti, B.F., "Sustainability assessment of a giant bamboo plantation in Brazil: Exploring the influence of labour, time and space," *Journal of Cleaner Production*, 18(1), 2010; pp. 83–91.
While the assessment of bamboo production is itself worthwhile, the inclusion of ternary diagrams in this article is of particular interest as a means to more succinctly communicate the implications of emergy assessment.

Brown, M.T., and Ulgiati, S., "Emergy measures of carrying capacity to evaluate economic investments," *Population and Environment*, 22(5), 2001; pp. 471–501.
Based on an emergy assessment of a region's renewable emergy sources, regional non-renewable storages, and external purchased resources, the carrying capacity of a region is used to guide choices about economic investment.

Brown, M.T., Cohen, M.J., and Sweeney, S., "Predicting national sustainability: The convergence of energetic, economic and environmental realities," *Ecological Modelling*, 220(23), 2009; pp. 3424–3438.
The emergy yield ratios and environmental loading ratios of nations are used as indicators of national sustainability.

Holling, C.S., "Understanding the complexity of economic, ecological, and social systems," *Ecosystems*, 4(5), 2001; pp 390–405.
The focus is on the adaptive cycles of large scale systems. The key concept presented in this article is "panarchy," a representation of system hierarchies as a set of adaptive cycles. The article concludes by attempting thus to reconcile the term "sustainable development" in the context of panarchy.

Lomas, P.L., Alvarez, S., Rodriguez, M., and Montes, C., "Environmental accounting as a management tool in the Mediterranean context: The Spanish economy during the last 20 years," *Journal of Environmental Management*, 88(2), 2008; pp. 326–347.
This article is important to consider for its longer timescale and nationwide assessment. As such, it reveals much about a longer view of current state dynamics in economic and ecological terms.

Odum, H.T., "Energy, ecology, and economics," *Ambio*, 2(6), 1973; pp. 220–227.
Classic text on the relationship between economics and ecosystem analysis. It covers important concepts including the energetics of inflation and growth. This text offers 20 points for unifying energetic, economic, and ecological systems.

Odum, H.T., and Odum, E.P., "The energetic basis for valuation of ecosystem services," *Ecosystems*, 3(1), 2000; pp. 21–23.
Clear explication of ecologically driven derivations of value and market-driven derivations of value, with the aim to "'externalize the internalities'

to put the contributions of the economy on the same basis as the work of the environment."

Ukidwe, N.U., and Bakshi, B.R., "Thermodynamic accounting of ecosystem contribution to economic sectors with application to 1992 U.S. economy," *Environmental Science and Technology*, 38(18), 2004; pp. 4810–4827.

This article focuses on an analysis framework that aims to incorporate "natural capital" into economic valuation systems by thermodynamic input–output analysis. Like other discussions of the thermodynamics of large scale systems, the fundamental aim here is to internalize the externalities and real wealth of bio-geophysical resources that are absent in current economic valuations.

Ulgiati, S., Zucaro, A., and Franzese, P.P., "Shared wealth or nobody's land? The worth of natural capital and ecosystem services," *Ecological Economics*, 70(4), 2011; pp. 778–787.

Focuses on a donor-side evaluation of the "Commons" as a complement and supporting set of arguments for incorporating the work done by the biosphere into policy and economic choices.

Emergy analysis

Brown, M.T., and Herendeen, R.A., "Embodied energy analysis and emergy analysis: A comparative view," *Ecological Economics*, 19(3), 1996; pp. 219–235.

Early discussion of emergy analysis procedures and both its similarities to and differences from embodied energy analysis.

Brown, M.T., and Ulgiati, S., "Emergy evaluation of the biosphere and natural capital," *Ambio*, 28(6), 1999; pp. 486–493.

Coherent introduction to how emergy values the "Commons" and how the emergy methodology can relate the economy and help guide policy in a way that incorporates bio-geophysical inputs using a donor-value approach to system dynamics.

Brown, M.T., and Ulgiati, S., "Updated evaluation of exergy and emergy driving the geobiosphere: A review and refinement of the emergy baseline," *Ecological Modelling*, 221(20), 2010; pp. 2501–2508.

Important update of the global emergy baseline and tables of unit emergy values for a range of materials based on a recalculation of global energy flows.

Brown, M.T., Odum, H.T., and Jørgensen, S.E., "Energy hierarchy and transformity in the universe," *Ecological Modelling*, 178(1), 2004; pp. 17–28.
This article presents a range of correlations about energy systems propensities at a range of scales from more familiar ecological scales of consideration to astrophysics. In all cases, the energy systems share a set of consistent system behaviors.

Ingwersen, W.W., "Uncertainty characterization for emergy values," *Ecological Modelling*, 221(3), 2010; pp. 445–452.
This article both describes the uncertainty of unit emergy values and then provides a framework for incorporating uncertainty into emergy analysis.

Hau, J.L., and Bakshi, B.R., "Promise and problems of emergy analysis: Short communication," *Ecological Modelling*, 178(1), 2004; pp. 215–225.
An overview of common criticisms of the emergy concept and methodology. The article then aims to clarify a range of misconceptions about emergy.

Odum, H.T., "Maximum power and efficiency: A rebuttal," *Ecological Modelling*, 20(1), 1983; pp. 71–82.
Odum's response and clarification of several points related to maximum power concepts, as challenged by an article by William Silvert in 1982. It is often useful to read varied restatements of the same concepts by Odum to clarify understanding of the operative principles as he sees them. Likewise, it is useful to engage the debate about emergy methods.

Odum, H.T., "Self-organization, transformity, and information," *Science, New Series*, 242(4882) (Nov. 25), 1988; p. 1135.
A solid summary of emergy analysis that ultimately focuses on the important role of information and humans as key sources of feedback in energy systems.

Odum, H.T., *Ecological and General Systems: An Introduction to Systems Ecology*, Colorado University Press, 1994.

Essential text that proposes the principles of maximum power systems. Introduces the emergy accounting methodology.

Odum, H.T., "Self-organization and maximum empower," in C.A.S., Hall, ed., *Maximum Power: The Ideas and Applications of H.T. Odum*, Colorado University Press, 1995; pp. 311–330.
One of Odum's more direct and clear statements about the maximum power concept.

Odum, H.T., *Environmental Accounting: Emergy and Environmental Decision Making*, New York: Wiley, 1996.
Applies the emergy methodology to a range of scales, types, and periods of energy systems: From economics to fuels, development alternatives, nations, and, information.

Odum, H.T., *Prosperous Way Down*, Boulder, CO: The University of Colorado Press, 2001.
H.T. Odum's final book focused on strategies for a future with declining petroleum sources.

Odum, H.T., *Environment Power and Society for the Twenty First Century: The Hierarchy of Energy*, New York: Columbia University Press, 2007.
Classic text that focuses on the role of power in socio-environmental systems.

Tilley, D.R., "Howard T. Odum's contribution of the laws of energy," *Ecological Modelling*, 178(1), 2004; pp. 121–125.
Succinct summary of Odum's primary emergy concepts and his proposals for the fourth, fifth, and sixth laws of thermodynamics.

Efficiency vs. efficacy

Jevons, W.S. *The Coal Question*, 2nd ed., London: Macmillan and Co., 1886.
This book proposed that increases in efficiency of resource use tend also to increase the consumption rate of that resource. In short, many efficiency measures tend to follow a logic of negated efficiencies.

Jørgensen, S.E. "The thermodynamic concept: Exergy," in S.E. Jørgensen, ed., *Thermodynamics and Ecological Modeling*, Boca Raton, FL: Lewis Publishers, 2000.

This chapter includes a cogent distinction between energy and exergy, and, by extension, of energy efficiency and exergy efficiency.

Kay, J.J., "Complexity theory, exergy, and industrial ecology," in C. J. Kilbert, J. Sendzimir, and G.B. Guy, eds. *Construction Ecology: Nature as the Basis of Green Buildings*, London: Spon Press, 2002; pp. 72–107.
This chapter includes many fundamental observations about energy systems, including the seemingly paradoxical role that energy efficiency plays in non-linear, non-equilibrium energy systems.

Odum, H.T., and Pinkerton, R.C., "Time's speed regulator: The optimum efficiency for maximum power output in physical and biological systems," *American Scientist*, 43(2), 1955; pp. 331–343.
Important discussion on the role of efficiency in energy systems. The authors emphasize the difference between maximum efficiency and optimal efficiency that yields maximum power.

Exergy analysis

Bastianoni, S., Pulselli, F.M., and Rustici, M., "Exergy versus emergy flow in ecosystems: Is there an order in maximizations?," *Ecological Indicators*, 6(1), 2006; pp. 58–62.
Parallel consideration of maximal exergy and maximal emergy, suggesting a chronological ordering to the two system propensities.

Bendoricchio, G., and Jørgensen, S.E., "Exergy as goal function of ecosystems dynamic," *Ecological Modelling*, 102(1), 1997; pp. 5–15.

Dincer, Ibrahim, and Rosen, Marc, *EXERGY, Second Edition: Energy, Environment and Sustainable Development*, Elsevier Science, 2012.

Jørgensen, S.E., Nielsen, S.N., and Mejer, H., "Emergy, environ, exergy and ecological modelling," *Ecological Modelling*, 77(2), 1995; pp. 99–109.

Schmidt, D., "Low exergy systems for high-performance buildings and communities," *Energy and Buildings*, 41(3), 2009; pp. 331–336.
Sound introduction to exergy concepts as they relate to buildings, for example the consequential distinction between energy efficiency and exergy efficiency. One example of a typical German house that is 70 percent energy efficiency but only 10 percent exergy efficient.

Sciubba, E., and Ulgiati, S., "Emergy and exergy analyses: Complementary methods or irreducible ideological options?" *Energy*, 30(10), 2005; pp. 1953–1988.

Shukuya, Masanori, *Exergy: Theory and Applications in the Built Environment*, Springer, 2012.

Slesser, M., Odum, H.T., and Huettner, D.A., "Energy analysis," *Science*, 196(4287), 1977; pp. 259–262.

Torío, H.A., Angelotti, A., and Schmidt, D., "Exergy analysis of renewable energy-based climatisation systems for buildings: A critical view," *Energy and Buildings*, 41(3), 2009; pp. 248–271.
Comprehensive review of exergy studies and methodologies related to varied building conditioning (heating, cooling) systems.

Fuel / power source evaluation

Beck, T.B., Quigley, M.F., and Martin, J.F., "Emergy evaluation of food production in urban residential landscapes," *Urban Ecosystems*, 5(3), 2001; pp. 187–207.
This article focuses on an emergy evaluation of four typical urban food production plots. In all cases, the high economic inputs of the production systems result in very low emergy yield ratios (between 0.0003 and 0.17), far from the break-even point of 1. Even over a five-year period that would begin to amortize the purchased inputs, the emergy yield ratios remain low.

Brown, M.T. and Ulgiati, S., "Emergy evaluations and environmental loading of electricity production systems," *Journal of Cleaner Production*, 10(4), 2002; pp. 321–334.
This article focuses on the emergy evaluation of six different electricity production facilities. The emergy yield ratio of hydroelectric and wind-based facilities is the highest, while oil-based thermal facilities are the lowest.

Brown, M.T., Protano, G., and Ulgiati, S., "Assessing geobiosphere work of generating global reserves of coal, crude oil, and natural gas," *Ecological Modelling*, 222(3), 2010; pp. 879–887.

Emergy assessment of the geophysical and biosphere work required to produce various fossil fuels.

Cavalett, O. and E. Ortega. E., "Integrated environmental assessment of biodiesel production from soybean in Brazil," *Journal of Cleaner Production*, 18(1), 2010; pp. 55–70.
This emergy assessment of biofuel production in Brazil reveals the low emergy yield ratio of biodiesel production (1.62), largely due to the direct and indirect resources required of its production. Accordingly, the "fraction of fuel that can actually be considered renewable is very low (around 31%)."

Franzese, P.P., Rydberg, T., Russo, G.F., and Ulgiati, S., "Sustainable biomass production: A comparison between Gross Energy Requirement and Emergy Synthesis methods," *Ecological Indicators*, 9(5), 2009; pp. 959–970.
Useful comparison of energy analysis (Gross Energy Requirement) and emergy analysis in the context of biomass production. The authors conclude that the two approaches are very different systems in the end and offer very different modes of evaluation.

Martin, J.F., Diemont, S.A.W., Powell, E., Stanton, M., and Levy-Tacher, S., "Evaluating and comparing the sustainability of three agricultural methods with emergy analysis," *Agriculture, Ecosystems & Environment*, 115, 2006; pp. 128–140.
Useful comparison of three farm types as assessed in terms of emergy yield ratios, environmental loading ratios, and emergy sustainability indices. It is instructive to compare more landscape-based evaluation examples in relation to buildings.

Paoli, C., Vasallo, P., and Fabiano, M., "Solar power: An approach to transformity evaluation," *Ecological Engineering*, 34, 2008; pp. 191–206.
Emergy evaluation of solar thermal and photovoltaic systems, compared against traditional energy transformation systems. In this study, emergy yield ratios remain quite low, near 1.

Pizzigallo, A.C.I., Granai C., and Borsa, S., "The joint use of LCA and emergy evaluation for the analysis of two Italian wine farms," *Journal of Environmental Management*, 86(2), 2008; pp. 396–406.
Comparison of "organic" and semi-industrial wine production processes as measured by a combined use of life cycle assessment and emergy analysis.

Rydberg, T., and Jansen, J., "Comparison of horse and tractor traction using emergy analysis," *Ecological Engineering*, 19(1), 2002; pp. 13–28.
Compelling comparison of mechanical and non-mechanical forms of traction. The article reveals that horse traction in 1927 had about 60 percent renewable inputs, whereas tractor traction in 1996 only had about 9 percent renewable inputs.

Brief historiography of emergy, maximum power, and their implications

Boltzmann, L. "The second law of thermodynamics," in *Theoretical Physics and Philosophical Problems*, B. McGuinness, ed., trans. P. Foulkes, Dordrecht, Holland: D. Reidel, 1974.
Boltzmann had a central insight that ultimately led to the development of emergy analysis. He observed that the struggle for existence was not a struggle for matter or energy, both of which are abundantly available, but rather a struggle for entropy. This construal of life helped introduce the concept of energy quality that is so central to the purpose and methodology of emergy analysis.

Brown, M.T., and Ulgiati, S., "Energy quality, emergy, and transformity: H.T. Odum's contributions to quantifying and understanding systems," *Ecological Modelling*, 178(1), 2004; pp. 201–213.
Useful historical summary of the energy quality and net energy concepts that preceded the emergy concept.

Georgescu-Roegen, N., *The Entropy Law and the Economic Process*, Cambridge, MA: Harvard University Press, 1999.
An attempt to position economic processes relative to the second law of thermodynamics with mixed results.

Kangas, P., "The role of passive electrical analogs in H.T. Odum's systems thinking," *Ecological Modelling*, 178(1), 2004; pp. 101–105.
Discussion of how electrical systems in part shaped Odum's system thoughts and diagrams. At the same time, it reveals how Odum's systemic thinking exceeded that on the more linear electrical analogues.

Kleidon, A., Lorenz, R.D., eds., *Non-equilibrium Thermodynamics and the Production of Entropy: Life, Earth, and Beyond*, Berlin: Springer, 2005.
Broad consideration of the maximum entropy production principles in the context of bio-geophysical contexts.

Lotka, A.J., "Contributions to the energetics of evolution," *Proceedings of the National Academy of Science*, 8(6), 1922; pp. 147–151.
Essential article on the development of the maximum power principle.

Popper, K., "On clouds and clocks," *Objective Knowledge: An Evolutionary Approach*, Oxford Press, 1972.
Philosophical reflection on systems perceived as either more deterministic "clocks" or as less deterministic "clouds." There is a focus on "plastic controls" in systems. In the explicitly quantitative methodology, it is important to recall that emergy analysis, like any form of energy analysis, is not deterministic. The analysis informs and guides actions but should not over-determine.

Prigogine, I., and Stengers, I., *Order Out of Chaos*, Toronto: Bantam Books, 1984.
Seminal introductory text on the thermodynamics of non-equilibrium and far-from-equilibrium systems. It includes a history of thermodynamic thought that led to the evolution of thermodynamics from equilibrium-based systems to non-equilibrium-based systems.

Schneider, E.D., and Kay, J.J., "Life as a manifestation of the second law of thermodynamics," *Mathematical and Computer Modelling*, 19(6–8), 1994; pp. 25–48.
This important article extends the observations about the struggle of life from Boltzmann and Lotka. These ecologists table several further observations about the role of energy in open, non-equilibrium systems.

Schneider, E.D., and Kay, J.J., "Complexity and thermodynamics: Towards a new ecology," *Futures*, 26(6), 1994; pp. 626–647.
Non-equilibrium consideration of open thermodynamic systems. It is asserted that systems should evolve to increase dissipation (i.e. do more work) through increased autocatalytic structure and form.

Schrödinger, E., *What is Life?*, Cambridge: Cambridge University Press, 10th ed., 2003.
Canonical text that triggered much work in this section of the bibliography on non-equilibrium, largely based on the proposition of the negentopy ("negative entropy") concept introduced in this text.

Thomson, W. (Lord Kelvin), "On the dynamical theory of heat," in W.F. Magie, ed., *The Second Law of Thermodynamics*, New York: Harper, 1899.
Kelvin's important statement regarding the second law.

Ulanowicz, R.E. *The Ascendant Perspective*, Columbia University Press, 1997.

Ulanowicz, R.E., and Hannon, B.M., "Life and the production of entropy," *Proceedings of the Royal Society*, London Series B, Biological Sciences, 232(1267), 1987; pp. 181–192.
This article is focused on the role of entropy production in biotic systems through a series of propositions.

Maximum power

Cai, T.T., Olsen, T.W., and Campbell, D.E., "Maximum (em)power: A foundational principle linking man and nature," *Ecological Modelling*, 178(1), 2004; pp. 115–119.

Cai, T.T., Montague, C.L., and Davis, J.S., "The maximum power principle: An empirical investigation," *Ecological Modelling*, 190(3), 2006; pp. 317–335.

Hall, C.A.S., "The continuing importance of maximum power," *Ecological Modelling*, 178(1), 2004; pp. 107–113.

Ulgiati, S., Bargigli, S., and Raugei, M., "An emergy evaluation of complexity, information and technology, towards maximum power and zero emissions," *Journal of Cleaner Production*, 15(13–14), 2007; pp. 1359–1372.
This article considers joint emergy evaluation and life cycle assessment as qualitative and quantitative assessments in a maximum empower/ "zero-emission" framework.

Pulsing

Allen, Timothy F.H., "Applying the principles of ecological emergence in building design and construction," in Charles J. Kilbert, Ja Sendzimir, and G. Bradley Guy, eds., *Construction Ecology: Nature as the Basis of Green Buildings*, London: Spon Press, 2002; pp. 108–126.

Holling, C. S., "The resilience of terrestrial ecosystems: Local surprise and global change," in *Sustainable Development in the Biosphere*, W.M. Clark and R.E. Munn, eds., Cambridge: Cambridge University Press; pp. 292–320.

Odum, H.T. "Pulsing, power and hierarchy," in W.J. Mitsch, R.K. Ragade, R.W. Bosserman, and J.A. Dillon, Jr., eds., *Energetics and Systems*, Ann Arbor, MI: Ann Arbor Science, 1992; pp. 33–59.

Odum, W.E., Odum, E.P., and Odum, H.T., "Nature's pulsing paradigm," *Estuaries*, 18(4), 1995; pp. 547–555.
Early discussion of Odum's pulsing concept applied to compare tidal salt marshes, tidal freshwater marshes, and seasonally flooded freshwater wetlands. It suggests that coupled internal and external pulsing of systems optimizes performance of the systems.

Richardson, J.R., and Odum, H.T., "Power and a pulsing production model," in W.J. Mitsch and J.M. Klopatek, eds., *Energy and Ecological Modelling: Developments in Environmental Modelling 1*, New York: Elsevier Scientific Publishing Co., 1981; pp. 641–648.

Regional assessments

Ascione, M., Campanella, L., Cherubinic, F., and Ulgiati, S., "Environmental driving forces of urban growth and development: An emergy-based assessment of the city of Rome, Italy," *Landscape and Urban Planning*, 93(3), 2009; pp. 238–249.
It is enlightening to expand the system boundary of an emergy assessment to a major city like Rome. The resulting assessment of Rome is then compared against other city assessments such as San Juan, Taipei, and Macao.

Agostinho, F., DinizG., Siche, R., and Ortega, E., "The use of emergy assessment and the Geographical Information System in the diagnosis of small family farms in Brazil," *Ecological Modelling*, 210(1), 2008; pp. 37–57.
Emergy methodology assessment of organic and chemical-based farms in Brazil, ultimately validating organic methods while in so doing identifying opportunities to amplify the various emergy-based indices. This article also is an example that integrates a GIS methodology as a means to help direct more regional scale policy questions.

Bastianoni, S., Marchettini, N., Panzieri, M., and Tiezzi, E., "Sustainability assessment of a farm in the Chianti area (Italy)," *Journal of Cleaner Production*, 9(4), 2001; pp. 365–373.
Comparison of different farm types and grape types to determine the relative long-term sustainability of the different argoecological techniques and farm outputs.

Brown, M.T., and McClanahan, T., "Emergy analysis perspectives of Thailand and Mekong River dam proposals," *Ecological Modeling*, 91(1), 1996; pp. 105–130.

Campbell, D.E., "Emergy analysis of human carrying capacity and regional sustainability: An example using the state of Maine," *Environmental Monitoring and Assessment*, 51(1), 1998; pp. 531–569.
Focuses on state-wide carrying capacity using an emergy assessment and compares the resulting emergy indices of Maine against other states such as Florida, Texas, and the United States. Advocates for a much stronger reliance on local, rather than purchased, inputs, given resources available in Maine.

Comar, V., "Applying H.T. Odum's concepts and principles in developing countries," Ecological Modelling, 178(1), 2004; pp. 171–175.

Federici, M., Ulgiati, S., Verdesca, D., and Basosi, R., "Efficiency and sustainability indicators for passenger and commodities transportation systems: The case of Siena, Italy," Ecological Indicators, 3(3), 2003; pp. 155–169.
The varied transportation systems of Siena are analyzed in terms of mass flow, revealing the varied efficacy of different modes (auto, bus, or train for people and materials).

Ferreya, C., and Brown, M.T., "Emergy perspectives on the Argentine economy during the 20th century: A tale of natural resources, exports and external debt," *International Journal of Environment and Sustainable Development*, 6(1), 2007; pp. 17–35.

Huang, S., and Hsu, W., "Material flow analysis and emergy evaluation of Taipei's urban construction," *Landscape and Urban Planning*, 63(2), 2003; pp. 61–64.
Useful analysis of Taipei's overall construction material mass flow along several indices as indicators of urban metabolism. This article offers insight into the impending "peak-sand" dynamic of the region.

Huang, S., Lee, C., and Chen, C., "Socioeconomic metabolism in Taiwan – Emergy synthesis versus material flow analysis," *Resources, Conservation and Recycling*, 48(2), 2006; pp. 166–196.

Lagerberg, C., and Brown, M.T., "Improving agricultural sustainability: The case of Swedish greenhouse tomatoes," *The Journal of Cleaner Production*, 7(6), 1999; pp. 421–434.
Emergy assessment of greenhouse-grown tomatoes that use different fuel sources (oil versus wood), as compared against field-grown tomatoes. The cost of inputs for the density of greenhouse production should shift to more renewable inputs.

Lefroy, E., and Rydberg, T., "Emergy evaluation of three cropping systems in southwestern Australia," *Ecological Modelling*, 161(3), 2003; pp. 193–209.

Lu, H., Campbell, D.E., Li, Z., and Ren, H., "Emergy synthesis of an agro-forest restoration system in lower subtropical China," *Ecological Engineering*, 27(3), 2006; pp. 175–192.

Lu, H., Kang, W., Campbell, D., Ren, H., Tan, Y., Feng, R., Luo, J., and Chen, F., "Emergy and economic evaluations of four fruit production systems on reclaimed wetlands surrounding the Pearl River Estuary, China," *Ecological Engineering*, 35(12), 2009; pp. 1743–1757.

Martin, J.F., "Emergy valuation of diversions of river water to marshes in the Mississippi River Delta," *Ecological Engineering*, 18(3), 2002; pp. 265–286.

Compelling emergy assessment of various hydrological dynamics in southern Louisiana. The introduction of elevated levees has resulted in the loss of sediments and nutrients from the Mississippi River to the Mississippi Delta. Proposed diversion of river water to the delta result in high emergy yield ratios in this study.

Pulselli, R.M., "Integrating emergy evaluation and geographic information systems for monitoring resource use in the Abruzzo region (Italy)," *Journal of Environmental Management*, 91(11), 2010; pp. 2349–2357.
Documents a regional emergy evaluation assessment using GIS (geographic information system).

Pulselli, R.M., Pulselli, F.M., and Rustica, M., "Emergy accounting of the Province of Siena: Towards a thermodynamic geography for regional studies," *Journal of Environmental Management*, 86, 2008; pp. 342–353.
This article presents the results of a regional emergy analysis regarding population, material, and energy systems. There is a focus on the role of local and non-local inputs as an indicator of system performance.

Rotolo, C.G., Rydberg, T., Lieblein, G., and Francis, C., "Emergy evaluation of grazing cattle in Argentina's Pampas," *Agriculture, Ecosystems and Environment*, 119, 2007; pp. 383–395.

Rydberg, T., and Haden, A.C., "Emergy of Denmark and Danish agriculture: Assessing the influence of changing resource availability on the organization of agriculture and society," *Agriculture, Ecosystems and Environment*, 117, 2006; pp. 145–158.

Ulgiati, S., Odum, H.T., and Bastianoni, S., "Emergy use, environmental loading and sustainability: An emergy analysis of Italy," *Ecological Modelling*, 73(3), 1994; pp. 215–268.
A national scale emergy evaluation of Italy based on a comparison of a range of thermodynamic and economic indicators.

Ulgiati, S., Odum, H.T., and Bastianoni, S., "Emergy analysis of Italian agricultural system: The role of energy quality and environmental inputs," in L. Bonati, U. Cosentino, M. Lasagni, G. Moro, D. Pitea, and A. Schiraldi, eds., *Trends in Ecological Physical Chemistry, Proceedings of the 2nd International Workshop on Ecological Physical Chemistry*, Elsevier, NY, 2002; pp. 187–215.

Vassallo, P., Paoli, C., Tilley, D.R., and Fabiano, M., "Energy and resource basis of an Italian coastal resort region integrated using emergy synthesis," *Journal of Environmental Management*, 91, 2009; pp. 277–289.
Regional emergy assessment in the context of tourism-dominated economy and the vulnerability of such economies due to high external non-renewable resource flux.

Yan, M.C., and Odum, H.T., *An Energy Evaluation of Tibet*, University of Florida, Gainesville: Center for Environmental Policy, 1996.

Yan, M.C., and Odum, H.T., "An emergy evaluation of the seven years' development of Qingyanzhou Ecological Experimental Station," *Journal of Chinese Geography*, 8(3), 1998; pp. 221–236.

Thermodynamic indicators

Bastianoni, S. "Use of thermodynamic orientors to assess the efficiency of ecosystems: A case study in the Lagoon of Venice," *The Scientific World Journal*, 2, 2002; pp. 255–260.

Bastianoni, S., and Marchettini, N., "Emergy / exergy ratio as a measure of the level of organization of systems," *Ecological Modelling* 99(1), 1997; pp. 33–40.

Brown, M.T., and Buranakarn, V., "Emergy indices and ratios for sustainable material cycles and recycle options," *Resources, Conservation and Recycling*, 38(1), 2003; pp. 1–22.

Brown, M.T., and Ulgiati, S., "Emergy-based indices and ratios to evaluate sustainability: Monitoring economies and technology toward environmentally sound innovation," *Ecological Engineering*, 9(1), 1997; pp. 51–69.

Brown, M.T., Hall, C.A.S., and Wackernagel, M., "Comparative estimates of sustainability," in C.A.S. Hall, ed., *Quantifying Sustainable Development*, London: Academic Press, 2000; pp. 695–714.

Tonon, S., Brown, M.T., Luchi, F., Mirandola, A., Stoppato, A., and Ulgiati, S., "An integrated assessment of energy conversion processes by means of thermodynamic, economic and environmental parameters," *Energy*, 31(1), 2006; pp. 149–163.

Ulgiati, S., Ascione, M., Zucaro, A., Campanella, L., "Emergy-based complexity measures in natural and social systems," *Ecological Indicators*, 11(5), 2011; pp. 1185–1190.

Ulgiati, S., Brown, M.T., Bastianoni, S., and Marchettini, N., "Emergy based indices and ratios to evaluate the sustainable use of resources," *Ecological Engineering*, 5(4), 1996; pp. 497–517.

Ulgiati, S., Odum, H.T., and Bastianoni, S., "Emergy use, environmental loading and sustainability: An emergy analysis of Italy," *Ecological Modelling*, 73(3), 1994; pp. 215–268.

Index